WOMEN IN ARCHITECTURE

a contemporary perspective

CLARE LORENZ

"Women are not yet part of the inner circle.
Fortunately, special architectural knowledge is not
secret, or cannot be hidden today. However, it is still
controlled by a select male few. So my struggle, and
that of other women, continues."

Beverly Willis

WOMEN IN
ARCHITECTURE

a contemporary perspective

CLARE LORENZ

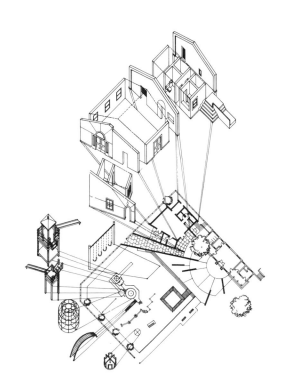

RIZZOLI
NEW YORK

To Christopher, William and Katharine

First published in the United States of America in 1990
by Rizzoli International Publications, Inc.
300 Park Avenue South, New York, NY 10010

Library of Congress Cataloguing-in-Publication Data
Lorenz, Clare
    Women in architecture / Clare Lorenz
        p.   cm.
    Includes bibliographical references.
    ISBN 0-8478-1277-4
    1. Women architects – Biography – History and criticism
    2. Architecture, Modern – 20th century. I Title.
    NA 1997.L67 1990
    720'.82 - dc20   90-52973
                                                      CIP
Book & jacket design: Linda Wade
Set in 9/11 Century by OTS Typesetting, Caterham
Printed and bound in Portugal

Contents

The country shown is current work/home base, not origin.

Notes and Acknowledgements

I am enormously grateful to a large body of people from many countries who have pointed me in the right direction, patiently answered questions and allowed themselves to be sounding boards when an outsider's judgement was required.

Without this body of knowledge and encouragement it would not have been possible to include contributions from so many parts of the world, for once embarked on research for this book I discovered how little previous study had been undertaken on the work of international contemporary women architects.

Was it a conspiracy of silence, or lack of interest on the part of architectural publications, or was it reticence (or inefficiency) in promoting work on the part of the architects themselves? This volume is far too slim to do justice to the work of all, or to cover every country in the world, but if it draws attention to the breadth of work undertaken by women architects by showing who has done 'what, where and when', then time will have been well spent.

Many thanks go to the following individuals and organizations for their particular help and kindness:
Charlotte Benton, Ruth Blum, Veronica Brinton, Peter Cook, Catherine Cooke, Liz McQuiston and Deanne Wildsmith, from Britain.
Clare James and Karin Mattson Nordin, from Sweden.
Wendy Evans, Mary McLeod, and Jane Thompson, from the USA.
Beatriz Wakeley and Luz Amorcho, from Colombia.
Yvonne Brunhammer, Anne Chaveau and Ignacio Gomez, from France.
Helena Iglesias Rodriguez, from Spain.
Nick Waterlow and Joan MacIntyre, from Australia.
Diana Lee-Smith, from Kenya.
Michael LLoyd, from Norway.
Romi Khosla, from India.
Catherine Muller-Schmid, from Switzerland.
Paloma Poveda of *El Croquis*, Spain.
Heather Olley of the Royal Australian Institute of Architects. Kenneth Forder of the Architects Registration Council of the United Kingdom. Laura Katz of the International Archive of Women in Architecture, USA. Millie Riley of the A.I.A. Archive of Women in Architecture, USA. Vincent Nacey of the Royal Institute of British Architects. Edouard Le Maistre of the Architectural Association, Britain. Phyllis Lambert of the Canadian Centre for Architecture.

Photographic Credits

p24-25: Brantenberg, Brantenberg and Hiorthoy, Norway. p26-27: Archives Municipales, Aubervilliers, France. p30-33: British Architectural Library, R.I.B.A., London. p40-41: Tim Hursley. p42-43: HSB, Sweden. p44-47: External of Studio House, Cervin Robinson courtesy of "House Beautiful"; Long Island House and Advertising agency, Norman McGrath; Architect's photograph, John Naar. p52-55: Kodak Headquarters, Lars Mongs; Keno Gard, the Globe and Triangular office, Jan Jordaan. The Globe facade, Elizabeth Hatz. p62-63: Wohnen am Volkspark, Berlin, Hans Theo Wagner. p66-69: Chester Road residences, Mosman Bay Marina and residence; Willem Rethmeier; Property resources office, Simon Cowling. p78-79: Mazingira Institute, Nairobi. p80-81: Arlington International Racecourse, John Craib-Cox; Boston Globe at Billerica, Nick Wheeler. p88-91: Grabo bay windows, Raymond Zielenski; The Triangle project before renovation, Per Jyllnor; after renovation, Lars Hasselrot; Courtyard at Ringaren, Hans Bowman; Architect's photograph, Hans Eric Brinkborg. p96-99: Seaside, Frank Martinez; Socol House. Scott Hedges; Villa Nova House, Raoul Pedroso; Clay House, Elizabeth Plater-Zyberk; Hibiscus House, Stephen Brooke. p104-105: Anita Niesz. p109-111: Banco de Credito, Tim Hursley; Centre for Innovative Technology, Tim Hursley; North Dade Justice Centre, Paul Warhol and Pat Fisher. p114-117: Royal Victoria Docks, Benjamin Thompson Associates; Faneuil Hall Market Place, Steve Rosenthal for Benjamin Thompson Associates; Ghiradelli Square, Jane Lidz for Benjamin Thompson Associates; Old Post Office, Washington, H. Hambright for Benjamin Thompson Associates; Union Station, Washington, Steve Rosenthal and Gregory Murphey for Benjamin Thompson Associates. p118-119: Arnold School, Nottinghamshire, British Architectural Library, R.I.B.A., London p120-123: Law Offices, Norman McGrath; Clark House and Fire station Five, Tim Hursley; Private residence, Amagansett, Elliott Kaufman; Iron Workers Union Headquarters, James Horner. p130-133: Lineflyg Headquarters, Jan Jordaan. p134-137: San Francisco Ballet Building exterior, Jane Lidz; interior, Beverly Willis; curved glass facade, Peter Aaron.

Introduction

'*Are* there any leading women architects?' an ignorant enquirer asked me as I approached the end of a year's research for this book. I am happy to report that indeed there are, more in some parts of the world than others, and that the number is growing. Far too often in the past inadequate credit has been given to, or demanded by, women architects and thus there continues to be, generation after generation, an element of surprise in their achievements.

'Is it possible to tell whether a building has been designed by a woman or a man?' was another question which raised its head a number of times. Some of the women in this book would reply 'No, of course not. The gender of the architect is quite irrelevant.' While strongly maintaining that they should be judged by their architectural work, others would argue that the two sexes have fundamental differences of approach to design, and that women should recognize their own value in what is still predominantly a man's world, and use it consciously in the search for a more humane architecture.

That is a refreshing view. Architects the world over are sometimes thought to be an argumentative group of inward looking professionals, pre-occupied with their own artistry above all else.

This book is a celebration of the work of contemporary women architects from twenty different nation states. So far as is known there has been little or no previous research in the field of contemporary, international women architects, and such a slim volume cannot attempt to provide all the answers. However it can place on record the achievements, breadth of interest and involvement in all aspects of architecture of four dozen women whose training has led them to propose a wealth of exciting solutions in widely differing fields. The choice was mine alone, and was far from haphazard.

The focus on individuals may appear curious as virtually all architectural work is that of a team, in that more than one individual contributes to the final product; only that work in which a woman has either led the design team, or been an equal partner or sole practitioner, is included. Each person's work, be it building, teaching or theory, is highly regarded in her own country, and the respect she has earned at home is the basis for inclusion here.

In some cases there were women I would have liked to include, but was unable to for certain specific reasons; the infirmity of old age (Charlotte Perriand, France) or the unrelenting pressure of work (Raili Pietila, Finland). On occasion politics and economics intervened. Information never materialized from China after the massacre in Beijing in the summer of 1989, and two South American architects, faced with unstable national economies, left for pastures new.

I have attempted to write for the reader who is interested in architecture, but holds no truck with the often arcane language used in many architectural books. In the main body of the book statements from the architects themselves are interwoven with my commentary. There is also a small section of statistics at the end which offers the reader the opportunity to make international comparisons.

The theme which has brought contributors together in this volume is above all one of good architecture, appreciated in its home country. The fascination in drawing together work from so many parts of the world lies in attempting to understand the context within which each architect works; the nation, its cultural background and both economic and climatic limitations. The range of work is wide, for what might be possible in the free market economies of the West might well prove unsuitable, or impossible, in less wealthy socialist states or developing countries. These points are implicit in the work of each contributor, whether or not they are openly referred to.

Sensibility and sensitivity to national and climatic conditions is evident throughout the book, together with cultural patterns: Swedish long term commitment to, and continuing development of, publicly funded housing; the American segmenting of an architect's job into 'design', 'marketing' or 'management' packages; the Australian attempt to define a national architecture suitable for the climate; or the unsure emergence of private practice in the USSR. Eulie Chowdhury, from India, writes of the problems of trying to solve the conflicting requirements of the Punjab climate. 'There is a variation of nearly 40 degrees Fahrenheit between day and night temperatures some days, and a range of between 0 and 118 degrees during the year. The climate is punishing. I wish someone could invent a kind of floating plastic umbrella over a city which could reduce the heat of summer and the bitter cold of winter.'

Whether in developing countries such as India, or in the developed world, there are still comparatively few women trained and practicing as architects. In many countries this contrasts strongly with other areas of the design field, such as interior, graphic, textile and fashion design. The number of practicing women architects is increasing rapidly in many parts of the world, but women architects as a percentage of the total still remain firmly in the minority everywhere.

In 1983 in Australia, where women architects were thought to constitute 3% of the total in 1989, they and others connected to the building industry banded together to form a support group called 'Constructive Women'. Its purpose was to build self-confidence through group discussion, and disseminate its views about the profession. It is interesting to note that the originator of the group feels that only 3% is 'critical mass'.

In stark contrast are the Nordic countries. Here there has been a long tradition of women working as architects, and the equivalent percentage rises to just under 20%. Swedish, Danish, Norwegian and Finnish women architects feel at ease in the society in which they work, and 'Athena', a Swedish women architects' group, exists more as a social club, taking groups abroad to visit places of interest, than as a support group. It is interesting that in the United States, the land of freedom and opportunity, which regards both architecture and issues of gender equality as areas of high profile discussion, the proportion of registered women architects is no more than 5%. According to the available statistics, this is similar to Spain. Who would have thought that Uncle Sam could boast no higher a proportion of female architects than a patriarchal Mediterranean society where opportunities for advancement might have been thought to be minimal?

It would be pleasing to think that nowadays anyone, anywhere, with the requisite training could openly practise as an architect without fear of discrimination. However, quite a number of contributors mentioned a period during their training or working lives in which they had felt disquiet or alienation as a result of expectations about them as 'women'. Sadly, discomfiture of this kind often seems part of practicing as a woman architect. Perhaps such problems are an occupational hazard for any body of people which has traditionally been in so small a minority compared with the dominant group.

'Dominance' is a word from which Birgit Cold, the Norwegian architect, would shy away. Her years of research have taught her to argue that men and women have different approaches to architecture and that these can be quantified and should be appreciated.

Eve Laron, from Australia, takes Cold's research further and argues that unless a woman's viewpoint is heard more loudly in the profession there is little hope for a better built environment. Laron talks of an architect's duty to serve the 'end user' well, and sees this as common to many women's approach to design.

This point is made in a number of different ways by such a large number of contributors, that it genuinely appears to go beyond that often stated, but too seldom meant, tenet of good architecture - that it should be responsive to the user's need. (A point often confused with the needs of the client, who may well commission a building, but never use it). Direct evidence of concern for the user shows especially in the work undertaken by two architects who have chosen to work in strongly contrasting areas. Madhu Sarin, in India, has put her training and talents to exemplary use among the poorest communities in her own country, and Jane Thompson, U.S.A., repeatedly proves her skill in revitalizing urban spaces the world over, to which the public flocks.

In the last resort this is what matters: the success of a building judged by its users - not, as is the norm in architectural circles, by other members of the profession, its critics or learned journals, who all too often appear to ignore the user and praise design solutions which reflect the architect's or client's egos.

Eve Laron's experience on becoming a partner may appear extreme - two male colleagues walked out in protest at this promotion of a female - but the Royal Australian Institute of Architects 1986 report to the Human Rights Commission on women in the architectural profession states that 'at least 54% reported sex-based attacks on their professionalism.' Lest anyone is tempted to think that Australia may be out of step with countries elsewhere, they should heed the conclusion from a 1989 survey of American architects undertaken for the magazine *Progressive Architecture*: 'In the field of architecture women are offered fewer opportunities and receive less compensation (salary), professional opportunities, recognition and rewards than do men with similar experience, say both our female and male respondents. At best, in a very few situations, respondents feel that women get equal treatment to men, but almost never do they feel women get better treatment, and overall women feel even more pessimistic than men about their situation. It may be that men are simply not aware that women face additional barriers.'

Consider after all the difficulties faced by the two courageous contributors who were among the first group of students to complete training on an equal footing to men in Saudi Arabia.

As discussion with contributors deepened, I found that a number of interesting attitudes towards the profession emerged. All were based upon direct experience, strongly felt, and tended to fall into age, rather than nationality, categories. A member of the first group - in her fifties or older - could appropriately be called *That Exceptional One*, to borrow the title of late 1980s exhibition about American women architects. She was enough of a rarity that, in being the odd one out, her curiosity value gave her a certain freedom. Beverly Willis, an American architect in her sixties, reflects on the manner in which she tumbled into architecture: 'My father was the first generation that did not homestead. Willis generations before him had pioneered into the western wilderness, cleared the land... and farmed. They were self-reliant country people with little education or cultural sophistication. I was in my twenties before I ever heard the word architect, or indeed met one.'

'Architecture is a cultural art whose foundation is the knowledge and tradition that has evolved over centuries..... the tragedy for me when I was young is that I did not even know that all this existed. Not knowing this, I did not know what questions to ask, let alone how to find the answers.'

She concludes somewhat bleakly, 'Women are not yet part of the inner circle. Fortunately, special architectural knowledge is not secret, or cannot be hidden today. However, it is still controlled by a select male few. So my struggle and that of other women continues.'

In descending age, the next group of architects are those who trained during the early 1970s when the feminist movement was at its most vocal. They are in their forties. They were at the start of the architectural schools' change in attitude towards the training of women. During the 1970s, and particularly from the mid-1980s onwards, the number of women entering training rose significantly. At the Architectural Association School of Architecture in London, the entry figure for first year women students rose from 14% in 1976 to 31% in 1986 and 48% in 1987. At the Bergen School of Architecture in Norway, 64% of the 1988 intake was women.

This was the generation of architects which took it for granted that it could do anything it wanted to, but had not allowed for the slowness with which society changes. It hoped there would be no struggle, but faced the realities of prejudice on and off site. In the main it overcame them.

The final, and youngest group of architects, are those in their mid to late thirties with no more than ten years practice behind them. In other professions this might be seen as long enough for patterns and attitudes to work to have developed. Not so in architecture, which, by the nature of its length of training, together with the time taken to reach seniority or build up a practice, means that recognition is rare until a decade after finishing training.

This group, far larger than those of previous generations, is fiercely determined to succeed, and will inevitably offer itself as role model for future generations. This is clearly needed. In 1989 only 48% of women architects in the *Progressive Architecture* poll had met, or knew, a woman architect before starting training. Virtually all men knew a male architect. As yet the age group has not shown sufficient staying power, in what is still predominantly a man's world, to convince the sceptics that women architects will really play an increasingly important role in the 1990s and beyond. It is also noteworthy that recent surveys of practicing architects show that, for a number of reasons, women's earnings are on average 75% of their male colleagues.

The older members of this same age group could now be expected to be reaching senior positions in large, internationally acclaimed firms. Very few have done so, and of those who have reached the top, many have subsequently left to set up practices which reflect their own values and approach to architecture. The younger generation of architects will continue to find, that despite an increase in numbers, little will change in the profession unless it effectively challenges the right to be employed on equal terms.

The architects selected for this book have brought all types of private and public building to my attention. There is not room to illustrate every example, but the pages which follow include fast track commercial work for developers, sometimes involving the master planning of vast acreages. It also contains the individual masterpiece, be it a factory, prison, office, library, school, or self-build house. I have tried, out of curiosity, to find areas or categories of work in which women have not, as yet, contributed fully to architecture. After much research I can only report that I have not yet come across designs for a munitions factory.

Clare Lorenz,
London, February 1990

USA Diana Agrest

Biography
Born in Argentina, now living and working in New York.
Obtained her Diploma of Architecture at the School of Architecture and Urbanism, University of Buenos Aires in 1967.
Post-graduate studies at the Ecole Pratique des Hautes Etudes at the Sorbonne and the Centre de Recherche d'Urbanisme in Paris from 1967-9.
Agrest is a partner in the firm A & G Development Consultants, Inc, New York, previously known as Agrest and Gandelsonas. Her work with the firm has been in the design and development of projects and buildings in the USA and other countries, ranging from single family houses and interiors to urban design and master plan proposals.
Agrest develops her teaching and theories on the relationship between architecture and the city concurrently with her building projects.
She is Professor of Architecture at Cooper Union, New York, where she has taught since 1976, and Adjunct Professor of Architecture at Columbia University, New York, since 1985.
She taught at Princeton University from 1971-5 and in 1988 was a visiting Professor there.
Fellow at the Institute for Architecture and Urban Studies in New York, 1972-1984, where she was the Director of the Advanced Design Workshop in Architecture and Urban Form.
She was Bishop Professor at Yale University School of Architecture in 1983.
She was the United States member of the jury for the international competition for the renewal of Les Halles, Paris.
Selected Work:
Three buildings in Buenos Aires, Argentina, 1984.

Diana Agrest, a partner in the firm A & G Development Consultants, works in central New York City where she combines teaching at Cooper Union and Columbia University Schools of Architecture with an increasingly busy practice.

Her buildings, which result from many years of thought and study about the nature of architectural design in cities, are a clear response to the city which she adopted after leaving Argentina in 1967 and having done postgraduate study in France at the Sorbonne and the Centre for Urban Research.

Her New York buildings are powerful, strong statements - and they need to be in this noisy city where people and buildings jostle and compete with an awe inspiring ferocity. Unlike the internationally acclaimed architect Philip Johnson, who designed a much publicized post-modern, pedimented skyscraper in central New York, Agrest cannot be safely labelled as a follower of a particular design philosophy, for although there is a strong hallmark to her buildings it comes through the use of common features rather than adherence to a set of prescribed rules.

From 1978-84 the practice designed a number of mixed use buildings in New York City which owe allegiance to the simplicity of the modern movement but are clearly designs of the late seventies and early eighties, with their deep set windows and double or triple height entrances. The severe, unornamented exteriors are a strong presence on the street but give no clue as to the way in which the building is used by its occupants.

By the late eighties, while maintaining her interest and skill in designing and manipulating double height spaces, Agrest shows great certainty in the use of materials and colour to create psychological warmth, as, for example, in the interior design of a duplex apartment in New York.

In her teaching, writing and urban planning work Agrest has always been fascinated by the relationship of city buildings with their urban context, and she has pursued this side of her work successfully at home and abroad. She was awarded second prize in a competition for a master plan for renewal of La Villette on the outskirts of Paris, and asked by the Milan Triennale to develop proposals for thirty acres of the Porta Vittoria area of Milan. Nearer home, in 1986 she produced proposals for a master plan for the development of Deep Ellum in Texas.

Agrest's influence on other members of the profession is considerable. As a New Yorker she lives and breathes the excitement which surrounds the architectural and design professions in this vibrant American city and contributes to

Building in Buenos Aires, 1977-82

the debate through her writing, teaching and lecturing. She was invited to represent the U.S.A. on the international competition judging panel for the renewal of the Les Halles area of central Paris, in which Richard Rogers and Renzo Piano built the controversial Pompidou Centre, and has been a jury member for the assessment panel of the American Academy in Rome.

Shingle-Schinkel holiday house, 1984. Two-pavilion house, 1984. Renovation of a Gramercy Park condominium building, New York, 1985. Four office interiors, 1985. Master plan proposals for Deep Ellum, Dallas, Texas, 1986. Bill Robinson Showroom, New York, 1986. West Street Office building, New York, 1986. Invited to develop thirty acres of the Porta Vittoria area of Milan, Italy, by the Milano Triennale, 1987.

Awards:

Second prize in the international competition for the urban renewal of La Villette outside Paris, 1986. She has been jury member for the Brunner Award and for the American Academy in Rome.

Her work has been widely published both at home and abroad. She has written extensively about architecture and there are over 100 articles about her work written by others.

She has written and published two books, one on the work of Irwin Chanin, the other a collection of her essays.

She is currently working on a book about the work of Agrest and Gandelsonas covering the period 1970-1985.

Duplex apartment.
Double height interior.

Colombia   Cecilia Alvarez and Emese de Murcia

Biography
Cecilia Alvarez Pereira.
Educated at the University
of Javeriana school of
architecture, Colombia,
1953-8. Registered
architect, 1950. Further
studies in population
planning, building
organisation, urban planning
and squatter communities in
Spain and Colombia
between 1962 and 1972.
Partner since 1972 in the
firm Alvarez Ijjasz Murcia
Ltd, Bogota, Colombia.
1957-64 architect with the
firms Guillermo Gonzalez
Zueleta and Pizano Pradilla
and Caro.
1964-79 at the Instituto
Credito Territorial (Institute
of Land Development)
working with the
Departments of Works,
Special Projects and Urban
Politics. She was
responsible for the design
and construction of more
than 2, 000 dwellings and
for surveying, developing
and implementing plans for
housing in deprived areas.
These dwellings, each
averaging 25 square
metres, were built in 35
cities in Colombia.
Emese Ijjasz De Murcia
Educated at the National
University, Argentina,
1956-8, Catholic University,
Santiago, Chile, 1958-61,
National University of
Colombia at Medellin,
Colombia, 1962. Registered
architect, 1963. Further
studies in housing and
planning, 1963. Member of
the Colombian Society of
Architects.
Senior partner in Alvarez
Ijjasz Murcia Ltd, Bogota,
Colombia, since its
inception in 1972. Upon
qualifying Emese de Murcia
worked in Medellin for an
engineering and
construction firm, 1962-3,
then joined the Instituto
Credito Territorial from
1964-71. During this period
she was responsible for the
design and construction of
over 17,000 dwellings.
From 1972-5 she worked
as a regional and urban

Emese Ijjasz de Murcia is the senior partner of Alvarez Ijjasz Murcia limited, an architectural practice opened with Cecilia Alvarez Pereira in 1972 in Bogota, Colombia.

Like other Colombian architects, Alvarez and de Murcia owe a great debt to the leadership of Luz Amorocho, who has worked and taught in the country since 1946. In her early days Amorcho designed and built for a number of firms but from 1966 concentrated on study and teaching at the National University of Bogota. She is greatly admired by younger architects and is seen as the 'grand old woman' of Colombian architecture. Alvarez and de Murcia, trained a generation after Luz Amorocho, find themselves amongst a growing community of women architects, but life is not without its ups and downs.

The unsure economy in Colombia, as in many other South American countries, has made difficulties for architects. They face sudden shortages of work and aborted schemes in periods of economic upheaval or political unrest. Many have fled elsewhere, notably to North America, where they are able to develop and pursue a steady career.

Clear survival strategies are needed by those who remain, so while maintaining a flow of work in their joint names, Emese de Murcia and Cecilia Alvarez have also worked with other practices and for developers during the thirteen years their practice has been in existence.

Together they have renovated a medical centre in central Bogota, designed apartments, built municipal and private housing, and constructed offices. In 1981 they renovated the offices of a large transport company in Bogota and in 1983 undertook a housing feasibility study for the same client; one year later they were asked by the same company to design 250 apartments.

In 1979 Alvarez and de Murcia won a housing competition for the design of a large estate, known as NIZA VIII, in the Niza area on the outskirts of Bogota, containing 684 apartments. Four years later they directed its construction.

Working with associate firms they have wrestled with urban planning and transport projects for the city authorities, as well as raising consciousness of the need to preserve fine old buildings and historic quarters of the city.

In 1985 they were asked to design over nine hundred apartments as the housing input to a massive development of an inter city passenger rail and road terminal in Bogota. Like much of their other high density, housing work, the scheme was no more than five stories high, and great care was taken to design interesting external landscaped spaces. As with the NIZA VIII development, solar collectors were used for water heating and local brick specified.

planner followed by urban development work with the firm Jorge E. Murcia Barrero from 1974. During the period 1976-8 she worked with the Instituto Desarrollo Urbano (Institute for Urban Development) in Bogota. In 1978 she was made Vice Dean of the University of Los Andes, Bogota, where she has taught since 1970. Her research with the Instituto Desarrollo Urbano was published in 1977-8.

Selected work of Alvarez Ijjasz Murcia Ltd:
Teusaca residence, Bogota, 1973. Renovation of the offices of the Terminal de Transportes (Transport Company), Bogota, 1981. Development plans for the Intercity passenger terminal, Bogota, 1981. NIZA VIII, 684 apartments, Bogota, 1982-3. Commercial centre '20th of July', Bogota, 1983. Working drawings for new apartments in Bogota, 1983-4. Renovation of six houses for individual clients, 1983-. 250 apartments for the Terminal de Transportes, Bogota, 1984. Medical centre, Bogota, 1988. Consultant urban planner for the Bogota transport system, 1988.

Awards:
The firm has been placed in five housing design competitions, winning two and coming second in the remainder. The two winning designs, for a 47 dwelling scheme, 1971, and a much larger 684 apartment estate, 1979, have both been built.

NIZA VIII housing project, 684 apartments, Calle 127, Bogota. Large scale development of high density (134 dwellings per hectare) six storey, social housing. The architects' prize winning design is on the edge of Bogota. Care has been taken to relate the scheme to the semi-rural site by softening the impact of the buildings through extensive planting.

Left above:
NIZA VIII housing project, completed 1984. Banks of solar panels, invisible from street level, heat the water for each of the 58 apartment blocks.
Left below: Commercial Development, 20th July, Bogota. Interior.

Emese de Murcia has, in addition to running her firm, taught at the University of the Andes in Bogota since 1967 and in 1986 was invited to the University of Miami to speak about Aldo Rossi's work in Bogota. Cecilia Alvarez worked with the Instituto de Credito Territorial from 1966-79 on a large range of urban development plans for a number of cities in Colombia.

13

Hong Kong Joanlin Au

Biography
Born in Hong Kong in
1953.
Educated at the
Department of
Architecture, University of
Hong Kong, Bachelor of
Arts in Architectural
Studies, 1977, and Bachelor
of Architecture with
Distinction, 1979. While a
student she won the
Jardine, Henry Lo
Scholarship, 1977-8, and
the Cement Marketing
Prize, 1977. She also won
the Hong Kong University
Alumni prize in 1977. Hong
Kong Authorized Architect,
1987. Council member of
the Hong Kong Institute of
Architects, 1989-. Council
member of the Hong Kong
Association for the
Advancement of Science
and Technology, 1989-.
Joanlin Au joined Ho and
Partners Architects
Engineers and Development
Consultants in 1987 and
became a Director in 1988.
From 1980-2 she worked
with David Russell and
Associates in Hong Kong
where she worked on
projects in New Guinea and
the New Territories. From
1982-4 she worked in
London for J.S.Bonnington
and Partners before being
offered a position with
Foster Associates in Hong
Kong to work on the Hong
Kong and Shanghai Bank,
1984-7.
Selected works, 1987-90,
with Ho and Partners:
Staff quarters for the Royal
Hong Kong Jockey Club,
Happy Valley, Hong Kong.
Dyeing factory at Tuen
Mun, New Territories.
Service Apartments in
Kennedy Road, Hong
Kong. Private house in
Repulse Bay, Hong Kong.
Commercial development,
Hong Kong. Commercial
development at Shenzhen
railway station, China.
Commercial development,
Central Hong Kong.
Commercial and residential
development at Hongqiao
Lot 26, Shanghai, China.
Invited competition for

When not working, Joanlin Au often soars above Hong Kong
in a glider looking down at its gleaming towers and ferries
plying across Hong Kong bay, or roars through the dense
city traffic on her Suzuki motorbike.

As a Director of Ho and Partners she is responsible for
the development of commercial and educational centres in
Hong Kong and mainland China. As a Hong Kong born and
trained architect she understands the inevitable pressures
of fitting too many people into too small a space and the
resultant need for high density architectural solutions.

'Architecture in the Orient has always had an unique
character and style,' she states. 'Hong Kong has turned
itself into a commercial and financial centre and this has led
to an aggressive architectural style which can be seen in
Hong Kong's skyline and along its waterfront. It is basi-
cally an international style overwhelmed with speculation,
and blind to contemporary Chinese and oriental architecture. Everybody rushes to keep up with the pace of life and
little opportunity is left for deeper thought about architectural ideals.'

Joanlin Au believes that a renaissance is due in Hong Kong
and that architects are well equipped to cope with it.

'Hong Kong is the place for a unique culture to be re-
born. Being an architect you meet the high powered financial chief and the most humble worker on site, and it is this
exposure to such a wide range of people which anchors an
architect to the surrounding society.'

After a short period in the early eighties in London she
returned to Hong Kong to work for Norman Foster on the
Hong Kong and Shanghai Bank from 1984-6. When the job
was completed she stayed in Hong Kong to work for Ho
and Partners and started work for another prestigious client,
the Hong Kong Jockey Club, in Happy Valley, 1987-9. Her
re-development of five blocks of 35 year old buildings as
living quarters for staff at the club came as a surprise to
neighbours. The curved front facade is neo-classical but at
the rear it is unashamedly high-tech.

Further suprises followed. Her competition entry for the
development of a ten block area of Olympic Boulevard in
Los Angeles featured proposals for an office building sporting
the American Flag, hung vertically down the front facade
from floors one to twenty. Her proposals received a spon-
sor's commendation.

Olympic West Garden District, Los Angeles, U.S.A. Planning proposals for the Third University of Hong Kong, City Polytechnic of Hong Kong, and the renovation of Western Market, Hong Kong.
Awards:
Hong Kong Institute of Architects Certificate of Merit for De La Rue's printing factory in Taipo, New Territories, 1983.

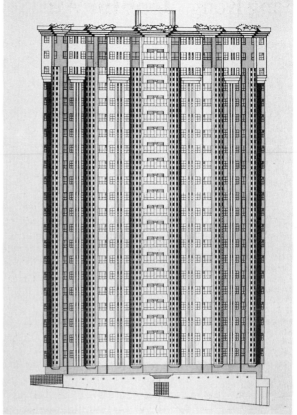

Above left: International Design Competition for Olympic West Garden, Los Angeles.
Above right: 58–70 Blue Pool Road, Hong Kong.

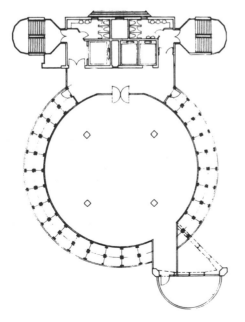

Left: Commercial Building in Tseun Wan.

Italy

Gae Aulenti

Biography
Born in Italy. Educated at
Milan Polytechnic Faculty
of Architecture, graduated
1954. Doctor of
Architecture.
Gae Aulenti works in Milan
running a practice which
includes architecture,
furniture design, stage
design, interiors and
domestic product design.
She was made an honorary
member of the American
Society of Industrial
Designers in 1967 and a
Chevalier of the Legion d'
Honneur in 1987 by the
President of France. In the
same year she was made a
Commander of the Order of
Arts and Letters by the
French Minister of Culture.
Merchandise Mart of
Chicago, U.S.A., conferred
the title of Dean of
Architecture, 1988. She
taught at the Faculties of
Architecture in Venice,
1960-2, and Milan, 1964-7,
and spent three years
researching with Luca
Ronconi, 1976-9, in
Florence. She has been on
the Board of Directors of
Lotus International
architecture and design
magazine since 1974.
Selected Work:
 Architecture. Holiday
Hotel, Trento, Italy, 1962.
Two elementary schools at
Meda, with Vico
Magistretti, 1967-9. Rodin
pavilion, Lugano,
Switzerland, 1970-1. Hotel,
Trieste, Italy, 1970-3. Villa
in Capalbio, Rome, 1971.
Restoration of the Chateau
de la Croe, Italy, 1972.
Villas in Parma, Pisa,
Parraggi, 1973. Villa in
Formentor, Spain, 1974.
Villa in Cap Ferrat, France,
1975. Residential buildings
in Caracas, Venezuela,
1977. Church in St Moritz,
Switzerland, 1978. Villa in
Perugia, Italy, 1978.
National Modern Art
Gallery at the Musée
d'Orsay, Paris, 1980-6.
Exhibition pavilion, Como,
Italy, 1983. Palazzo Grassi,
Venice, Italy, 1985. Museo

Gae Aulenti takes full advantage of the heady freedom allowed to architects in Italy to practice as designers in many different fields. Her firm forms part of the hub of a design network which feeds Italy's industrial powerbase in the north of the country. Designers from all over the world have flocked to Italy - more specifically to Milan - since the late sixties to satisfy the demands of design conscious industrialists, and to create and feed off the stimulating atmosphere of a city where design is seen as an integral part of daily life.

Gae Aulenti's work has staggering breadth; she designs almost everything. The Musée d'Orsay art gallery in Paris, palazzos in Venice, houses in Milan, offices in Rome, a museum in Barcelona and a bank in Bologna. She works on showrooms for prestigious international companies, such as Knoll International in the United States and Marina B in Switzerland. Her furniture, lamps, and sanitary fittings are to be found in the catalogues of Italy's most stylish companies and her 16 stage sets, 1975-88, have been seen in top opera houses such as La Scala in Milan and the Teatro dell' Opera in Rome.

Her name is linked to two of Italy's important industrial companies - Fiat and Olivetti. In 1970 she designed a travelling exhibition for Olivetti which went to six cities in France, Spain, Japan and Britain. Her work for Fiat stretches from 1968-1978 and encompasses showrooms in Turin and Brussels and two trade stands for the Turin Motor Show.

Her furniture and lamp designs stretch from 1968 to the present day. Knoll International asked her to design furniture for the company in 1971, 1976 and 1985, while Zanotta returned to her for three commissions for tables and chairs between 1964 and 1972. Artemide, one of Italy's most highly regarded lighting companies asked her to design six lamps between 1968 and 1975.

In 1988 she typically turned her attention to four different fields of interest. As an architect she built a racecourse in Pisa, a museum in Florence, renovated a palazzo in Rome and built a bank in Bologna. As an interior designer she designed an exhibition showing the history of the Fenice theatre in Venice and designed showrooms to be built in Los Angeles and St Louis for an Italian company.

In her role as stage designer she drew the sets for *Tsar Saltan* which travelled from the Theatre Romolo-Valli in Reggio-Emilia northwards to performances in Milan. On top of this she managed to slip in a series of lectures on America's West coast, and finally 1988 saw her head hunted by Louis Vuitton, the Parisian luggage company which persuaded her to design a watch and a pen and pencil set for its new range of products.

Palazzo Grassi, Venice. The Palazzo Grassi, on the Grand Canal, houses the Fiat art collection.

de l'Arte Catalana,
Barcelona, Spain, 1985.
Offices for Pirelli, Rome,
1986. Luis University,
Rome, 1987. College Citta
degli Studia, Biella, 1987.
San Rossore racecourse,
Pisa, 1988. Civic Museum,
Prato, Florence, 1988.
Palazzo Muti-Bussi, Rome,
1988. Palazzina della
Casiglia, Modena, 1988.
Bank Credito Emiliano,
Bologna, 1988. Interior
design: Max Mara offices
and showrooms, Milan,
1965. Olivetti showrooms
in Paris, 1966, Buenos
Aires, Argentina, 1967.
Knoll International
showrooms, New York and
Boston, U.S.A., 1969,
Milan, 1970. Three banks
in Milan and New York,
1971-3. Nine domestic
interiors in Milan, Genoa,
Rome, Turin and Paris,
1970-82. Fiat showrooms in
Turin and Brussels, 1970,
and motor show stands,
Turin, 1968 and 1976.
Mirabeau Restaurant,
Monte Carlo, 1973. Marina
B offices, Geneva, 1977,
New York, 1986. Boat
interior, 1984. Exhibition
designs, Venice, 1986 and
1988, Cremona, 1987.
Adrienne Vittadini shops in
St Louis and Los Angeles,
U.S.A., 1988. Furniture
and product design. Chair,
1962, and sofa, 1964, for
Poltronova, Italy. Tables
and chairs, 1964-72, for
Zanotta, Italy. Tables and
lamps, 1964-86, for
Fontana Arte, Italy. Tables
and other furniture, 1971-
85, for Knoll International,
Italy. Lamps, 1965-7, for
Martinelli Luce, Italy.
Lamp, 1967, for Candle,
Italy. Lamps, 1968-75, for
Artemide, Italy. Series of
furniture pieces, 1968 for
Kartell, Italy. Sanitary
fittings, 1973, for Ginori,
Italy. Door handles, 1977-
82, for Fusital, Italy.
Drawing board, 1980, for
Zucor and Bieffe, Italy. Tea
service, 1980, for Rossi
Arcandi, Italy. Sofa, 1986,
for B&B Italia, Italy.
Bench, 1987, for Ultima
Edizione, Italy. Sofa, 1988,
for Poltrona Frau, Italy.
Sanitary fittings, 1988, for
Ideal Standard, Italy.

Musee d'Orsay, Paris.
Interior, showing the picture display and high level temperature
control systems.

Watch, pen, pencil, fountain pen, 1988, for Louis Vuitton, Paris. Stage Design. Sets for opera and theatres in Naples, Genoa, Milan, Florence, Rome, Pesaro and Ravenna in Italy; Lyons, Nanterre, Paris in France and Munich in West Germany. 1975-88.
Awards:
Grand International Prize for the Italian Pavilion, 13th Triennale, Milan, 1967. First prize for elementary school design at Meda, with Vico Magistretti, 1967. Ubu prize for the best Italian Stage Design in 1978, Milan, 1980. Architecture Medal awarded by the French Academy of Architecture, Paris, France, 1983. Joseph Hoffmann prize for 1983 awarded by the Hochschule for Angewande Kunst, Vienna, Austria, 1984. The 16th Congress of the International Union of Architects (U.I.A.) nominated the Gare d'Orsay conversion as one of the ten most important works in the previous three years, 1987. Gae Aulenti has written many articles which have featured in *Casabella* and *Lotus* magazines and her work has been published in six books including *Gae Aulenti*, Electa, Milan, 1979, and *Gae Aulenti e il Museo d'Orsay*, Electa, Milan, 1987. She has been invited to lecture and speak at conferences in Spain, West Germany, Colombia, Canada, Iran, Sweden and the U.S.A. Her work has featured in exhibitions in Milan and at the Museum of Modern Art (M.O.M.A.), New York.

Interior. 19th century art collection.

Musée d'Orsay, Paris. The old Gare d'Orsay railway station
now houses one of France's national art collections.
The sculpture hall.

USA   Denise Scott Brown

Biography
Born in Zambia in 1931.
Educated at the
Architectural Association
school of architecture,
London, 1952-5, A.A.
Diploma, and the University
of Pennsylvania,
Philadelphia, Masters
degree in City Planning,
1960, and Masters Degree
in Architecture, 1965. She
is an Associate of the Royal
Institute of British
Architects, member of the
American Planning
Association, and Fellow of
Princeton University. She
has received honorary
doctorates from Oberlin
College, 1977, New Jersey
Institute of Technology,
1984, Parsons School of
Design, 1985, and
Philadelphia College of Art,
1985.
Denise Scott Brown is a
principal in the Philadelphia
practice, Venturi Scott
Brown and Associates,
where she has worked
since 1967. The firm is
known throughout the
world for its architecture,
city planning and urban
design, furniture and
interiors. It has received
more than 70 major awards
in the United States. Ms
Scott Brown has taught and
lectured extensively over
twenty years including a
five year teaching period as
an assistant professor from
1960-5 at the University of
Pennsylvania, followed by
three years at the
University of California in
Berkeley and Los Angeles,
1965-8. She is currently on
the board of directors of
the Urban affairs
partnership, Central
Philadelphia Development
Corporation, and the
Chestnut Hill Academy in
Philadelphia. Her extensive
writing on architectural and
planning issues includes a
1986 contribution to
*American Architecture:
Innovation and tradition*
published by Rizzoli, New
York, 1986. In 1987 she
received the
Commendatore of the

Denise Scott Brown is a principal in the Philadelphia based firm Venturi, Scott Brown and Associates. When she joined the firm in 1967 she added a new dimension to the practice - urban planning - and it is this which has remained her speciality.

'Over the last 20 years there have been numerous shifts in our practice based on demands and challenges presented by the clients,' she comments. 'I introduced a planning division into the firm, one grounded in urban design but progressing toward the social sciences on one side and more deeply into architecture on the other. We have also become involved in decorative arts, furniture design and exhibition design.'

'In the office I work at the same time on a number of different types of projects; for example, Dartmouth College, New Hampshire's plan to incorporate into its campus the adjacent complex of hospital and medical school buildings, the National Gallery extension in London, and the Philadelphia Orchestra hall...

I did not expect that I would become as involved as I have over the years in the management of our firm. Its special character, as an intensely knit, closely held organisation, given to design for the arts and for institutions, based to a considerable degree on idealism, and involving a mix of talented people, has caused Bob Venturi and me to become much more philosophical about organization and management than we had expected. I have found my planning training useful to develop strategies for this vulnerable organization over the years. This has involved knowledge of economics and financing as well as understanding of the changes in the demand for our services and the nature of our relationship with our clients on various projects. My studies in decision theory at Penn University really helped me with this.'

'I have over the years kept an arm's length relationship with teaching. My five intense years of full time teaching followed an urban planning course at the University of Pennsylvania when Louis Khan was teaching there - a period full of the theories of social scientists and the emergence of the civil rights movement. As a young professor at the University of Pennsylvania, Philadelphia, and then at Berkeley, California, I tried to meld the often conflicting forces of my South African background, English training and American planning studies. I was on the Massachusetts Institute of Technology's board of advisors for 10 years and currently teach a course at Harvard's Graduate School of Design in Cambridge, Massachusetts.'

'I see myself as an architect and planner whose window on the world is architecture, and whose field of most activity is urban design. I feel that I have a broad span, both in terms of an international background and among a number of disciplines as well. I enjoy the challenge of introducing perspectives from various fields of architecture and architectural expression.'

'The last few years have brought a new challenge as we have started work in Europe. My English schooling and meagre knowledge of Italian and French have been useful.'

'I enjoy equally helping to evolve an economic strategy for a metropolitan region, collaborating on the design of a museum, or working to the millimetre on the profile of a chair. On a recent three day weekend I spent the first day preparing for a job interview for the design of a museum campus in an American city, the second day outlining the introductory programme for my Harvard course 'The architecture of well being', and the third day writing a proposal for the redesign and rehabilitation of a dock area in a European city. Looking back on the third evening I couldn't think of a better, more challenging or more interesting way to spend a long weekend.'

Denise Scott Brown.

Order of Merit from Italy, and the Chicago Architecture award. She also holds five other awards given to her between 1977-86, and eleven awards for urban design and planning projects in the three year period 1980-3.

Selected work, 1985-: Renovation and change of use for part of Shippensburg University, Shippensburg, Philadelphia, 1985. Restoration of the antelope house at Philadelphia Zoo for a children's exhibition space, 1985. Adaption of Clothier Hall for a student centre, Swarthmore College, Philadelphia, 1985. Lewis Thomas Laboratory for Molecular Biology, Princeton University, 1985. Visitor centre and primates exhibit at Philadelphia Zoo, 1986. Stony Creek office centre, conversion of a brewery, Norristown, Pennsylvania, 1986. Restoration of the Fine Arts library at the University of Pennsylvania, Philadelphia, 1989-. Additions to the Thayer School of Engineering, Dartmouth College, New Hampshire, 1989-. Clinical research building for the University of Pennsylvania medical school, Philadelphia, 1989-. Additions to La Jolla Museum of Contemporary Art, La Jolla, California, 1989-. Medical research laboratory for the University of California at Los Angeles, 1989-. Centre for International Studies building at Princeton University, New Jersey, 1989-. Seattle Art Museum, Seattle, Washington, 1989-. Extension to the National Gallery, London, England, 1989-. Hall for the Philadelphia Orchestra, Philadelphia, 1989-. Denise Scott Brown has been a major contributor to 25 urban planning schemes since 1974 including the master plan for part of Austin, Texas, 1984, and a development plan for the centre of Memphis, Tennessee, 1987. She is currently working on redevelopment plans for an extension to Dartmouth College, New Hampshire, 1989-. She has been involved with the design of 12 exhibitions, including *High styles: 20th century American Design* at the Whitney Museum of American Art, New York, 1985. Ms Scott Brown has designed fabrics, china, glassware, wallpaper, jewelry and furniture for international companies including Knoll International and Alessi and Cleto Munari in Italy..

Street plan of Memphis, Tennessee.

Beale Street north side

Cotton Row west side

Cotton Row east side

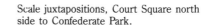

The Old Daisy Theatre, Beale Street, Memphis.

Scale juxtapositions, Court Square north side to Confederate Park.

Scale relationships are relative rather than absolute. The archway at the Old Daisy theatre would look small as an opening to Convention Hall; it looks large on Beale Street. Beale Street itself looks poignantly small, awash in its sea of parking and the Pinch looks diminutive half hidden behind the expressway. But the architecture of Cotton Row, although not very much larger in scale than that of Beale Street, looks considerably grander because of its still remaining urban context.
                    Denise Scott Brown.

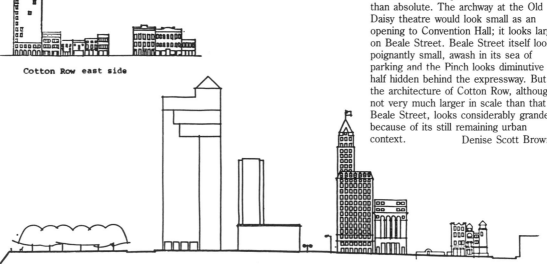

Eulie Chowdhury & Elizabeth Ghuman

Eulie Chowdhury and Elizabeth Ghuman have each played an important role in the development and training of architects in India today, and to assess their importance as pioneers one must place them in the historical context of India under colonial rule pre-1945, and after independence as a developing nation state.

Ghuman, as Scottish born wife of a British serving officer, found herself in India at the time of transition to independence and was called upon to provide assistance in training for architects in India. Chowdhury, who left India during the second world war to train in Australia, returned in the early fifties to work on the highly prestigious development of the Punjab's new capital, Chandigarh, and stayed to develop her career.

Elizabeth Ghuman was amongst the first intake of students reading architecture at Glasgow University before the second world war and spent a number of years working in Glasgow and the north of England before becoming the wife of a fellow student from Glasgow, who was then a British

army officer in India with the Royal Engineers. She reflects, 'I was an Army wife in Bengal and Bihar, then in New Delhi where my husband constructed roads, bridges and airstrips for the new sad war with our neighbours. To my surprise Maulana Azad, Minister of Education asked me to apply for the Headship of the Government School of Architecture in Delhi, and to my greater surprise I was appointed on a contract for five years, later extended by another three years.'

'Those eight years (1948-56) were very busy but very rewarding. Nearly all the students of this period, men and women, have become successful architects. One group was awarded the Aga Khan prize for the Moghul Sheraton in Agra. Raj Kumari Amrit Kaur, Minister of Health, gave me opportunity and appreciation; Indira Ghandi, as her father's daughter, before she became an over busy Prime Minister, was hospitable and co-operative, and Jane Drew (Senior Architect at Chandigarh in the early fifties) was generous in giving practical experience to the students.'

Eulie Chowdhury trained as an architect in Sydney, Aus-

Polytechnic for Women, Main block, Chandigarh.

in the Lothians for the British Government on Land Settlement schemes for ex-servicemen. She worked on education buildings in Leicester and during the second world war in clinics, air raid shelters and doing fire service. In 1944 she was a senior lecturer in Leeds and subsequently worked for the Ministry of Town and Country Planning, London. She taught at the Architectural Association immediately after the war for two years and went to India shortly thereafter.

She built Constantia Hall and hostel for the YWCA in New Delhi and designed houses for self-build clients. With her engineer husband she was responsible for laying fresh water pipes to remote villages in Himachel Pradesh. This was continued by the Indian Government's Public Works Department. In the Punjab she was asked to design a church and a home for retired people.

Hostel Block for the Home Science College, Chandigarh.

tralia, during the second world war and after a period in the United States returned to India in 1951 to work on Le Corbusier's plans for Chandigarh, the new Punjab capital. She was the first Indian woman to qualify as an architect and to be elected a Fellow of the Royal Institute of British Architects and Fellow of the Indian Institute of Architects.

From 1963-5 she was Principal of the Delhi School of Architecture and Planning, a position held previously by Elizabeth Ghuman, but returned to practice in 1966 becoming Chief Architect of Harayana State in 1970 and of the Punjab in 1976. She remained as Chief Architect in the Punjab until her retirement in 1981 and was responsible for the design and construction of all government buildings, the planning of new townships and the Thein Dam Project.

In the Punjab she was responsible for an enormously varied assortment of public buildings; from medical and educational buildings, industrial developments and sports centres, railway stations, tourist facilities and hotels, theatres, temples, police and fire stations, community centres, orphanages and leper colonies, circuit and state guest houses and housing for everyone from peons to a Raj. Not content with this formidable workload she continued to research and lecture in Delhi and Chandigarh and write official reports for the Punjab Government on conservation and transport problems.

Norway   # Birgit Cold

Birgit Cold.

Biography
Born in 1936. Educated at
the Royal Academy of Fine
Arts, School of
Architecture, Copenhagen,
Denmark. Architecture
degree, 1961. Dean of the
Department of Architecture
at the Norwegian Institute
of Technology at the
University of Trondheim
from 1986 and Professor at
the Division of Architectural
Design.
She has her own practice in
Trondheim, started with
partners Tore Brantenberg
and Edvard Hiorthoy in
1964. As an academic her
teaching, lecturing and
research have concentrated
on the evaluation of quality
in architecture. She taught
architecture at Trondheim
from 1963 and undertook
10 years of research for
the Foundation for Scientific
and Industrial Research,
Trondheim University,
1973-83. She was a council
member of the Norwegian
Research Council for
Applied Social Science,
1986-8, and of the Council
for Social Science Research
from 1982-4. She is a board
member of the Norwegian
Academy of Technical
Sciences, the European
Association of Architectural
Education and the
organisation 'Technology
and Human Values'. During
1987 she was a member of
the board of the Norwegian
Building Research Institute.
*Selected work with her
practice:*
10 private family houses,

Professor Birgit Cold is Dean of the Department of Architecture at the Norwegian Institute of Technology, part of Trondheim University. She has devoted many years of research to education at schools of architecture, where she has studied the nature of architectural teaching and called for improvements. She has also undertaken wider study in the field of general education and looked at the possibility of increased community use of school buildings. Her studies have taken her around Europe and to Japan, and she has been asked to speak at conferences in many countries.

Birgit Cold dismisses 'fashion' in architecture and constantly looks for architectural quality. She writes, 'The interactive battle between traditional and innovative forces is an exciting and stimulating fight which goes on continuously with special intensity during periods of change. The real fight is about the lack of quality when neither traditional nor innovative values are present. It happens when we are copying or repeating former expressions and forms without keeping the original character, construction and materials, but using less valuable, less refined and lasting solutions. It also happens when originality is overwhelmingly excessive and the more traditional values are put aside.'

'Training architects is not enough to increase quality in the built environment. A "Built Environment" programme should be offered to planners and the public to enable them to visualize, or be aware of, their surroundings. Education authorities must offer such programmes and schools should run them; architects must be responsible for sharing their skills and knowledge with people and designing functional and aesthetic environments for learning and development.'

Birgit Cold draws upon the research of two architects, one German, the other French, to consider 'balance' in society and architecture. She looks for an all-inclusive architecture which reflects the approach and aspirations of all members of society.

'A society dominated in the traditional sense by masculine principles is a society preferring exterior values such as prestige, power and monumentality, and is not one that attaches importance to feelings, care and love. Architecture has one foot in technology, one in social sciences and

Housing at Tjensvoll, Norway.

Norway, 1964-75. 1, 118 apartments for Trondheim Housing Association, Trondheim, 1970-75. Renovation of a kindergarten at Trondheim asylum, Trondheim, 1975. 8 terrace houses for Trondheim Housing Association, Trondheim, 1975. 282 terrace houses for Stavanger housing Association, Stavanger, 1976. 285 terrace houses for Kristiansand Housing Association, Kristiansand. *Awards:* Two first prizes for a town hall and social housing. Two second prizes for social housing. Three further awards for an exhibition hall, townscape and flexible housing. Her research has been published in 13 Norwegian publications and in 12 journals outside Norway.

the third in aesthetics; within this it is interesting to observe and analyze the female and male principles in design.'

'The German architect Margrit Kennedy has studied the feminine and masculine values in architecture. She stresses the importance of an all inclusive design process combining these values and for clarity sets out female principles alongside masculine ones:

More user orientated.......than designer orientated.
More ergonomic.............than monumental.
More functional.............than formal.
More flexible.................than fixed.
More organic orders........than abstract systems.
More user orientated.......than designer orientated.
More ergonomic.............than monumental.
More functional.............than formal.
More flexible.................than fixed.
More organic orders........than abstract systems.
More holistic.................than specialized.

More complex................than one dimensional.
More socially orientated...than profit orientated.
More slowly growing.......than quickly risen.'

'This is not a description of the *architecture* designed by female and male architects but it does describe different attitudes towards technology and nature, different ways of thinking and different interests. It gives all of us an opportunity to examine our feelings, sympathies, needs and work theories so that we may create a more all inclusive architecture which will fulfill human needs and dreams.'

Roumanian sketch.

25

France   Marina Devillers & Lena Perot

Biography
Marina Devillers.
Born in 1947 in Bucharest.
D.P.L.G. Diploma, 1971,
Master of Architecture
degree from the University
of Pennsylvania, U.S.A.,
1972. Planning licence,
Paris, 1972.
Teaching at the Ecole
d'Architecture, Belleville,
1988-9.
Lena Perot.
Born in 1945 in Bucharest.
D.P.L.G. Diploma, 1969,
Graduate diploma in Urban
Studies at the Institute for
Political Study, Paris, 1976.

Marina Devillers and Lena
Perot started practice
together in 1972 in Paris as
Marina Devillers and Lena
Perot, Architects. They
have specialized in housing,
mostly on the edges of
Paris and undertaken
research for the Ministry of
Urban Planning.
Selected Work:
17 dwellings and offices for
technical services,
Aubervilliers. 33 dwellings,
'La Maladrerie', Reims.
143 dwellings in the town
centre of Pierrefitte.
Sabatier School at Bobigny.
28 dwellings, 'La
Maladrerie', Reims.
Renovation of La
Maladrerie quarter of
Reims. 63 individual
dwellings, Cergy-Pontoise.
88 dwellings, Cergy-
Pontoise. 121 dwellings,
Chambery. 76 dwellings,
Aubervilliers. College in
Villepinte. 85 apartments
for port employees, 1989-.
Renovation and extension
of the Town Hall,
Aubervilliers. Proposal for
the planning of housing,
post office and parking in
the Bertinerie area of
Saran, Loiret. Research for
the Ministry of Town
Planning into public access
to municipal buildings,
1986. Proposal for the
Carrefour supermarket
chain at Bobigny.
Awards:
Competition prizes
for:secondary school at

Marina Devillers and Lena Perot, who are sisters, opened the doors of their Paris office in 1977.

In a short period of time they won a string of major awards for their entries to architectural competitions, and they undertook a formidable programme of housing projects and public buildings. Both were trained as urban planners, in addition to their architectural training. They have tackled problems of access to public buildings and, for the French Ministry of Urban Planning, the difficulties of extending the Paris metro line.

They comment, 'In the 1970s architectural competitions made their appearance in France. They gave our generation the opportunity to launch ourselves, especially in the field of social housing. Our first win, in 1977, led to the opening of our office with two social housing projects. The following twelve years have been filled with periods of encouragement and periods of difficulty - just like any other office.'

'We work almost exclusively with the State as our client and appreciate this situation. The brief does not represent the interests or the wishes of only one person, but of a group of people. This 'public brief' is offered mainly through architectural competitions and we have entered more than thirty in twelve years. This has allowed us to tackle a great variety of projects and to maintain the flow of design work, which is what should happen in an office! We enjoy the intense periods of thought and creativity which precede the final solution - and we always regret that we cannot spend longer on this stage - however the intensity of competition work is hard to keep up.'

'We find that people are astonished that two sisters work together, and comment on it. There are really no good answers to give them, except that our closeness leads to agreement on many things and eases the early stages of working out a scheme. Being sisters has helped a great deal on the main difficulty facing women architects: bringing up children with a working week more than one hundred hours long. Architecture certainly dictates our life, and we do not offer much resistance !'

At Pierrefitte Devillers and Perot faced the problems of inserting a new high density 143 apartment housing scheme, completed in 1987, between a vast 1960s ten storey development and the existing town.

They describe their approach to the design and comment on its reception by the occupants as follows: 'The idea was to create a system of streets, courts, alleys and buildings which could make a transition between high rise buildings and the old town of Pierrefitte. Also we thought it impor-

Reception area for the Technical Services Department at Aubervilliers Town Hall.

tant to increase the number of entrances and staircases in order to create small communities of neighbours to share these places and avoid damage to them. It works very well !'

Two other recent competition wins have kept the practice busy. The Town Hall administration building at Auber-villiers, which contains offices and exhibition and reception halls, was completed in 1988, and a school for 600 eleven to fourteen year olds at Villepinte is under construction in 1990.

Villepinte, 1988, 1500
apartments for port
employees, plans for the
town centre of Saran,
Loiret, 1987, Sabatier
school at Bobigny, 1982;
plans for the centre of
Drancy, 1980; town houses
for Cergy-Pontoise, 1976;
special jury prize for the
Place de la Halle, Sancerre.

Side facade of
Aubervilliers Town Hall.
143 dwellings at
Pierrefitte.

Aubervilliers Town Hall.

Saudi Arabia

Mona Khalid Al Dossary & Ghada Abdul Aziz Al-Mogren

Biography
Mona Khalid Al Dossary
Born in Al Khobar, 1965.
Educated at the College of
Architecture and Planning,
King Faisal University,
Dammam, graduated with
an honours degree,
Bachelor of Architecture
and Planning, 1987.
Awarded the Prince
Muhammad bin Fahad
Award for Scientific
Eminence in 1987.
Mona Khalid Al Dossary is
joint owner, with two
partners, of The Last Line
Est. which opened in 1988.
The establishment does
architectural work in
consultation with licensed
offices, interior design and
retails objets d'art. She is
one of the first intake of
women to be allowed to
train as architects in Saudi
Arabia. Training
commenced in 1982.
Selected Work:
Indoor swimming pool for
Sheik Al Khalifa at Riffa,
Bahrain, 1989-. Proposals
for a villa for Sheik Al
Thani, Doha, Qatar. Office
conversion, Al Khobar,
1988. Office renovation for
Khalid Al Dossary Est.,
1989. Proposals for a
confectionery shop, Al
Khobar, 1989-. Design
work. *Twenty Curtain
Designs* a book on curtain
styles, 1989. Posters on
different subjects, printed
in Kuwait and for sale in
Saudi Arabia, and
illustations for a health
guide, 1989.
*Ghada Abdul Aziz Al-
Mogren*
Educated at the College of
Architecture and Planning,
King Faisal University,
Dammam, graduating in
1987 with a Bachelor of
Architecture and Planning
degree.
Ghada Abdul Aziz Al-
Mogren is a teaching
assistant at the College of
Architecture where she
trained in Dammam. She
teaches all aspects of

Mona Khalid Al Dossary and Ghada Abdul Aziz Al-Mogren are two of Saudi Arabia's first women architects to be trained in the Kingdom. As part of the country's desire to educate men and women equally they were given the same opportunities as their male colleagues throughout the five year tuition period, 1982-7, and graduated with full qualifications to practice. Mona Al Dossary, a star pupil, was awarded the highly prestigious Prince Muhammad Bin Fahad Award for Scientific Eminence at the end of her training. Both women left college determined to work professionally, and to stay in Saudi Arabia. They have not found life on the outside easy.

'In Saudi culture men and women are separated due to social and religious customs,' writes Ghada Al-Mogren, who teaches at the college where she trained in Dammam. 'From primary school onwards male and female facilities are separate. Consequently, sometimes there are communication difficulties and it is easier for women to communicate with each other than with men. In the last few years women have started to appear in the workplace as the country develops; one such example is at the Riyadh Bank.'

'Currently women are expected to take an active role in developing the Kingdom. Increased employment opportunities for women are proposed in direct proportion to their better educational background'.

With thoughts of these impending changes in Saudi society, Ghada Al-Mogren designed a women's headquarters building on a site in Riyadh, the capital, as her thesis project in 1987. Sadly it is unlikely to be built, but the thought behind it is sound. She proposed that it be a meeting place where working women could discuss difficulties they might encounter and find the services they needed - medical care, banking and professional advice. It was suggested that the client be the women's branches of the Directorate for Female Education, the Civil Service Board, the Public Administration Institute, the Ministry of Labour and Social Affairs and the Riyadh Bank.

Mona Al Dossary is less sanguine about the position of women. She boldy states. 'I belong to the first generation of Saudi women architects; one can imagine what an alien idea it is here. I think that the toughest obstacle that my women colleagues have to face is to convince both client and employer of their abilities. During my relatively short career I have found that clients accept a woman architect far more easily than employers or fellow male architects. Employers try to bargain with the salary, while many men

Last Line Est., Al Khobar, 1988. Mona Al Dossary

think that a woman has no talent for business.'

She has clear views about architecture. 'Architecture is the only form of art that we live in instead of observe and I therefore approach it as the design of 3-D spaces. I believe that it is this which has given historic buildings their "quality value".'

'Our country's wealth has lead to importing foreign materials and these are often designed for climates far less harsh than ours. They restrict design possibilities and result in buildings which use a lot of energy. I believe we owe it to future generations, while we have the time and money, to develop materials and methods that suit the local climate and conserve energy.'

In 1988 she turned down the opportunity for further study in Abu Dhabi. 'I felt I had to, since the girls' department in the College of Architecture and Planning in Dammam stopped accepting more students. There was, and still is, lots of talk about it being shut altogether as most of the

Ghada Abdul Aziz
Al Mogren.

interior design and has
responsibilities on the
administration and
professional practice
committees.

Swimming pool for Sheik Al Khaliffa, Bahrain, 1989. Mona Al Dossary

graduates failed to find proper employment. It is true they work freelance, but that gives little job security and even less control over work quality.

Given these circumstances, and without (as yet) the necessary number of years experience to be licensed as consultant architects, Al Dossary and two colleagues opened their own business in Al-Khobar in 1988. They work together with established offices for 'full architectural work' and specialise in renovation work and interior design themselves. Being unsure whether this would prove financially viable they opened a showroom, attached to their office, selling paintings and handcrafted art objects. In October 1989 they celebrated their first year of business.

'We have great plans for the future, but we are in no hurry. We have to overcome many problems to get the quality work we aim at. All through this first year we have been learning about the availability of materials and craftsmanship in the market, and to our astonishment, about our own capabilities and talents.'

Britain   Jane Drew

Biography
Born in Thornton Heath,
Surrey, in 1911. Educated
at the Architectural
Association School of
Architecture, London,
1929-34. AA Diploma.
Fellow of the Royal
Institute of British
Architects. Honorary
Fellow of the American
Institute of Architects,
1978. Honorary Fellow of
the Nigerian Institute of
Architects, 1985. Honorary
Fellow of the Institute of
Contemporary Arts,
London. Honorary
doctorates from Ibadan
University, Nigeria, 1966,
the Open University,
Milton Keynes, 1973, and
Newcastle University,
1987.
Jane Drew worked with her
husband, Maxwell Fry,
from 1945-77 in Fry Drew
and Partners, London.
After completing training at
the A.A. Jane Drew
worked with J.T.Alliston
from 1934-9 and ran her
own practice during the
second world war, 1939-45.
She has worked at times
with Denys Lasdun,
Lindsey Drake, Norman
Creamer and Frank Knight
and is a consultant to Fry
Drew Knight Creamer,
Sevenoaks, Kent. She was
President of the
Architectural Association,
1970 and has been a
member of the Royal
Institute of British
Architects' Council. She
was a member of the
Victoria and Albert
Museum Advisory Board,
London and a member of
the Institute of Arbitrators
and the City of London
Advisory Committee for
Conservation areas. Jane
Drew designed a number of
exhibitions during her early
years in practice. Kitchen
planning exhibition, London,
1941, *Britain Can Make It*
at Olympia, London, 1942
and *Rebuilding Britain*, at
the National Gallery,
London, 1943.

Jane Drew.

Throughout a long career, until her retirement in 1978, Jane Drew was always to be found where the action was: debating in her deep and somewhat penetrating voice in Council at the Royal Institute of British Architects, discussing survival tactics for the Architectural Association in 1970 during her Presidency, or persuading her political left wing friends, amongst them the then Prime Minister, Michael Foot, of the necessity to open university education to all.

Her work, much of which has been in West Africa and the Indian continent, has won her fame and honour. Her position in the centre of an international world of architects and architectural debate for forty years continues to fascinate.

She was influenced by the MARS group - a group of architects, painters and industrialists who were responsible for the introduction of the modern movement into Britain and for offering temporary refuge to ex- Bauhaus figures Walter Gropius and Marcel Breuer when they fled Germany in the 1930s. At the same time she also listened to the international debates of CIAM, a group of architects from many European countries who were interested in discussing the social, political and architectural implications of the modern movement.

From 1951-4 she worked as a Senior Architect at Chandigarh, the new Punjab capital, supervising work for Le Corbusier and Pierre Jeanneret, and designing and building her own schemes such as the Government College for Women and the Government Higher Secondary school. In England at this time she was expected to wear a hat and gloves when meeting clients, but in India, as with all her other work abroad, she found a welcome freedom. She was responsible for the recruitment and training of all Indian staff and for the design and supervision of construction.

In West Africa, where she worked intermittently from 1947 to 1965, she showed sensitivity to local housing needs and suggested simple improvements which cost little. Her book on village housing in the tropics, written with Maxwell Fry and Harry Ford in 1947, was the start of her great interest in, and love for, the people and races of West Africa. From 1953-65 in Nigeria she built University buildings at Ibadan, facilities for the Co-operative Bank in Lagos and Ibadan, the Olympic stadium and swimming pool at Kaduna. In 1946-7 she built colleges and a girls school in Ghana, followed, in 1964, by a training centre.

In the late seventies she designed the *Suffragette and Suffragist* exhibition in the House of Commons with Jill Craigie. She was a consultant to the British Commonwealth Gas Corporation from 1941-3 designing kitchens for it and a town planning advisor to the Resident Minister for the West African Colonies from 1944-6. Jane Drew wrote a number of books in collaboration with other architects. *Architecture for Children* with Maxwell Fry, 1944, and a book on kitchen planning in the same year. She founded the *Architect's Year Book* in 1946 and was joint editor with Trevor Dannatt until 1962. She wrote *Village Housing in the Tropics* with Maxwell Fry and Harry Ford in 1947 and *Tropical Architecture in the Humid Zone* in 1956 with Maxwell Fry. Invited to teach as Beamis Professor at Massachusetts Institute of Technolgy (M.I.T.), 1961, Harvard Graduate School of Design, 1970 and Utah University, 1976.
Selected Work:
Housing in Winchester, 1939. Walton Yacht Works, Walton on Thames, 1940. Colleges in Ghana, 1946, with Maxwell Fry. Wesley Girls School, Ghana, 1947. Hospital building for Kuwait Oil Company, 1949-51. Passfields flats, Lewisham, London, with Maxwell Fry, 1950. Waterloo Bridge entrance tower and harbour bar restaurant for the Festival of Britain, London, 1951. Senior Architect for the new capital of Chandigarh, Punjab, India, 1951-4. Flats at Whitefield Lane, Lewisham, London, 1953. University College, Ibadan, Nigeria, with Maxwell Fry, 1953-9. Co-operative Bank, offices and shop, Lagos, Nigeria,1959. Co-operative Bank, assembly hall and maisonettes, Ibadan, Nigeria, 1959. Gulf House for Gulf Oil Company, London, 1959. Housing for oil company employees, Gach Saran, Iran, 1959. Lionel de Wint Art Centre,

Festival of Britain, Harbour Bar Restaurant, London, 1951.

Olympic stadium, Kaduna, Nigeria, 1965.

Colombo, Sri Lanka, 1960. Apowa training centre, Ghana, 1964. Institute of Contemporary Arts, London, 1964. Housing at Hatfield, Hertfordshire, 1964. Housing at Harlow, Essex, 1964. Housing at Welwyn, Hertfordshire, 1964. Shell Oil Company headquarters, Singapore, 1964. Olympic stadium and swimming pool, Kaduna,Nigeria, 1965. Hotel, Colombo, Sri Lanka, 1965. School for Deaf Children, Herne Hill, London, 1968. The Open University, Milton Keynes, Buckinghamshire, 1969-77. Carlton House Terrace Art Gallery. London, 1970. Torbay Hospital and Nurses residence, Torbay, Devon, 1973. Gestetner buildign,Stirling, Scotland, 1976. Institute of Education, Mauritius, with Maxwell Fry, 1977. Science block for St Paul's Girls School, London, 1978.

University College, Ibadan, Nigeria. Arts and Administration Tower, 1953-9. With Maxwell Fry.

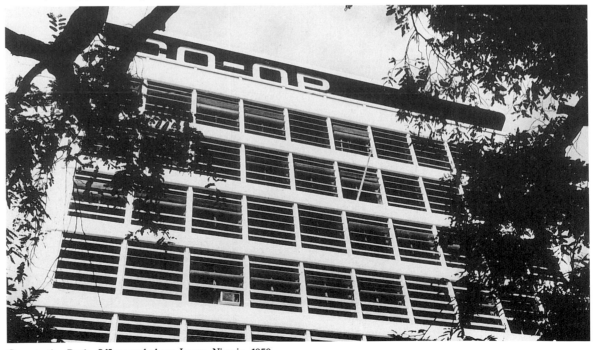

Co-operative Bank, Offices and shops Lagos, Nigeria, 1959.

After lengthy discussion in the early 1970s the British Government agreed to start a university open to everyone over the age of eighteen irrespective of their previous academic track record. Fry Drew and Partners were chosen as architects and Drew, to her great delight, saw the realization of her dream that university education should be available for all. The Open University was built on a green field site at Milton Keynes, a new town north west of London, between 1969 and 1977.

From 1970s onwards requests came from the United States for her to teach and, with a vast programme of building behind her, she took time away from the practice to do this. The honorary doctorates began to roll in, the latest received from Newcastle University in 1987.

Government College for Women, Chandigarh, India, 1951-4.

Holland

Magreet Duinker

Biography
Born in Holland in 1953.
Educated at the Technical
University, Delft, 1971-80.
Magreet Duinker is a
partner of Duinker, van der
Torre, Samenwerkende
Architekten, started in
Amsterdam in 1984. The
practice employs eight
people. From 1982-4 she
worked with three others in
a practice known as
D.T.B.B. on the
rehabilitation of a
nineteenth century housing
complex in Amsterdam, and
for two years prior to this
for S.W.S., Rotterdam,
1980-2. Teaching at the
Architecture faculty of the
Amsterdam Art School,
1988-.
Selected Work:
32 apartments in the
Jordaan, Amsterdam, 1987.
49 apartments in the
Dapperbuurt, Amsterdam,
1988. 97 apartments in Von
Zesenstraat, Dapperbuurt
Amsterdam, 1989-. 236
apartments on a new
housing estate in West
Amsterdam, 1990-. In
preparation; 64 apartments
in Kinkerbuurt,
Amsterdam; 210
apartments in The Hague.
Awards:
City Council of Amsterdam
prize for 49 dwellings in the
Dapperbuurt, Amsterdam,
1988. Magreet Duinker's
work has been published in
Bouw, 1987 and 1989, *de
Architekt*, 1989, and
*Architecture in the
Netherlands Yearbook*,
1988-9.

Magreet Duinker and her partner, Machiel van der Torre, run an Amsterdam practice devoted solely to social housing. Their prize winning scheme for forty nine dwellings on three small infill sites in the nineteenth century, red brick Dapperbuurt quarter of Amsterdam, is greatly admired by tenants and passers-by.

It pulls no punches, as Magreet Duinker is the first to admit; 'The design is not meant to adapt itself to the historic street facades or to people's historic or nostalgic preferences. The buildings have a transparent, clear and colourful prescence as independent structures in an existing street.'

'In the Dapperbuurt buildings the stairs are parallel to the front elevation - an alternative to the traditional Dutch stairwell. The idea was to create access that is not only used as an entrance to the dwellings but that also has a quality as an outdoor communal zone shared by two or three households.'

'For the neighbours opposite the building, and passers-by, the spectacle of residents and their visitors coming and going is a lively theatre'.

She continues, 'Qualities that are lacking in recent dwelling designs are spaciousness and flexibility. Criticism does not concern the overall size, but the way the dwelling is rigidly divided into small rooms, only fit for restricted activities.'

'Apart from spaciousness, the need for good daylight and a view out into the street or inner courtyard is even more important in a tightly knit city structure. From one's home one should be able to see the sky and trees, and experience the seasons and the weather changes. Large windows and diagonal views are important to attain these qualities.'

'We have developed two types of floor plans that meet these requirements; the 'sliding wall' dwelling, and the 'suite of rooms' dwelling.'

'The sliding wall dwelling is used in Wagenaar Straat. The bathroom and kitchen is organised in a small central unit, and around this lies a large free space which can be divided up with sliding walls. The width of the building reinforces the spatial effect. Daylight and sunlight penetrate deep into the apartments, and inhabitants use the plan in very different ways. Each individual dwelling has its own character and identity.'

Balconies at the rear of 30-36, Wagenaarstraat, Amsterdam, 1988.

Entrance stairwell, van Swindenstraat, Amsterdam, 1988.

19th century entrance stairwell, London.

Left: 3-13 van Swindenstraat, the Dapperburt, Amsterdam.

Axonometric, 30-36 Wagenaarstraat.

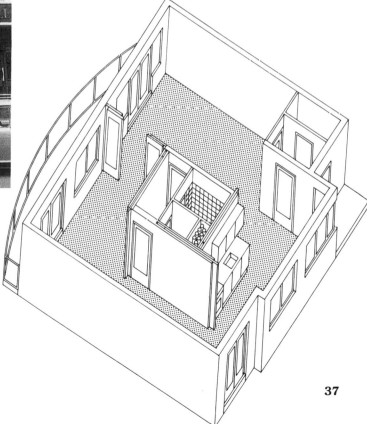

USA Merrill Elam

Biography
Born in Nashville,
Tennessee, in 1943.
Educated at Georgia
Institute of Technology,
Bachelor of architecture
degree, 1971, and Georgia
State University, Master of
Business Administration,
1982. Member of the
American Institute of
Architects.
Merrill Elam is a principal
in the Atlanta, Georgia,
based firm Scogin Elam and
Bray Architects which was
founded in 1984. Her work
covers a range of cultural
and commercial projects
together with long term
involvement with the
Highland Museum of Art,
Atlanta. From 1969 -1984
she worked for Heery &
Heery, Architects and
Engineers, becoming Vice
President in 1981.
*Selected built work with
Scogin Elam and Bray
includes:*
The High Museum at
Georgia -Pacific Centre,
Atlanta, Georgia, 1984.
Atlanta chamber of
commerce corporate
headquarters, Atlanta,
Georgia, 1985.
Headquarters building for
Clayton County Library,
Jonesboro, Georgia,1986.
Buckhead branch, Atlanta-
Fulton library, Atlanta,
Georgia, 1986. Gallery for
the Bureau of Cultural
Affairs, Atlanta City,
Atlanta, Georgia, 1987.
Herman Miller showroom,
Atlanta, Georgia, 1988.
The Candler School of
Theology, Emory
University, Atlanta,
Georgia, 1988. House
Chmar, Atlanta, Georgia,
1989. Morrow branch
Library, Clayton County
Library System, Morrow,
Georgia, 1989.
*Selected work with Heery &
Heery, Architects includes:*
Martin Luther King Junior
and Middle school,Atlanta,
Georgia, 1969. Crestwood
High School,Fulton County,
Georgia, 1971. Road
Atlanta auto racing facility,
Atlanta, Georgia 1972.

Merrill Elam works in Atlanta, Georgia, one of the Deep South states. She worked for Heery and Heery Architects in Atlanta for a fifteen year period, 1969-1984, rising to become Vice President of the firm in 1981. In 1984 she left to become a partner of the firm Scogin, Elam and Bray where she has been responsible for the practice's education and arts buildings.

While with Heery and Heery she was responsible for a wide range of buildings from local radio stations to schools in Atlanta, a county jail in Alabama and the Tallahassee City Hall in Florida.

She has always maintained a great interest and involvement in the visual and performing arts and in awakening children's interest in architecture - the latter through a series of exhibitions which she staged at the High Museum of Art. 1986 saw the opening of her design for a new public art gallery in central Atlanta called the High Museum at the Georgia-Pacific Centre. The museum is sited within an existing office development at the rear of the ground floor main lobby and auditorium. Merrill Elam chose a ramp as a central device in the design, both as a practical method of circulation and as a way of presenting differing eye level views of art works to the exhibition visitor.

At the Clayton County Library headquarters and branch library building, completed in 1988, Elam created low and high internal volumes by fanning the roofline out and upwards across the site. The roofline 'steps' which are thus created allow natural light to flood in over the bookstacks. The private administration area is connected to the public library by a joint reception area which - it being America - lies above a large car park.

Merril Elam

Both projects have won American Institue of Architects awards.

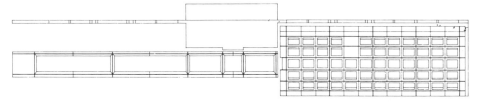

The High Museum at Georgia-Pacific Centre, Atlanta, Georgia, 1984.

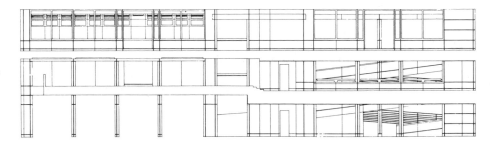

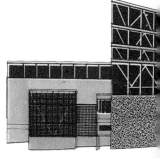

Shelby County Jail, Columbiana, Alabama, 1975. Woodruff Medical Centre, Emory University, Atlanta, Georgia, 1977. Georgia Power Company headquarters, Atlanta, Georgia, 1976. U.S. shoe headquarters, Cincinnati, Ohio, 1980. Tallahassee City Hall, Tallahassee, Florida, 1980. From 1974-1983 Elam contributed to seven exhibitions at the High Museum of Art, Atlanta, Georgia, in which varying aspects of architecture were introduced to children. Elam taught at Harvard Graduate School of Design, Massachusetts, 1987, Georgia Institute of Technology, Mississippi State University and Auburn University. She has lectured at conferences at academic institutions including Cranbrook Academy of Art, Michigan, and Harvard University, and addressed the Atlanta National Organization of Women in Construction. She is on the board of directors of the 'Room to Move 'dance company, Atlanta, and was founding member and president of the Architetcure Society of Atlanta in 1982. In that year she won a competition sponsored by the Atlanta Arts Festival and in 1983 was honour by Atlanta Women in film for her achievements in architecture. She is past president of the Georgia State board of Architects, a member of the Women in Architecture group and is on the membership committee and National committee on Design of the A.I.A. During the period 1984-7 she has been an adjudicator on ten award programmes and her work, from 1977 -1988 has been the subject of 23 articles.

Awards:
Clayton County headquarters library, A.I.A. South Atlantic region honor award High Museum at Georgia-Pacific Centre. A.I.A. National Honor and South Atlantic region honor awards. Urban Design Commission award of excellence, Gallery and Museum Association of Georgia Outstanding Museum award, 1986, Georgia Business Council for the Arts award. Tallahassee City Hall, Georgia Association A.I.A honor award. Radio headquarters and broadcasting facility, *Progressive Architecture* award. Georgia Association A.I.A. awards for two children's exhibitions *The City* and *Spaces and Illusions*.

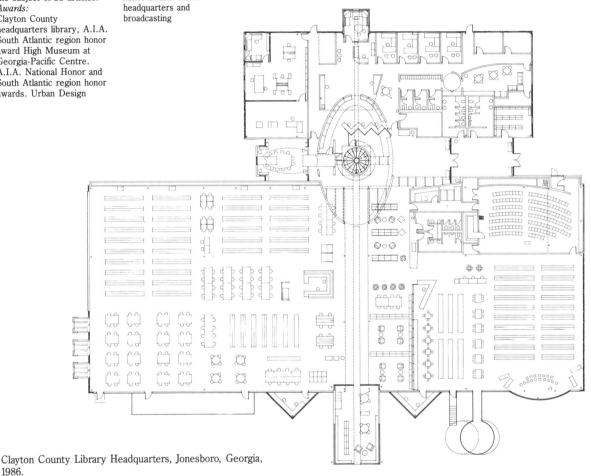

Clayton County Library Headquarters, Jonesboro, Georgia, 1986.

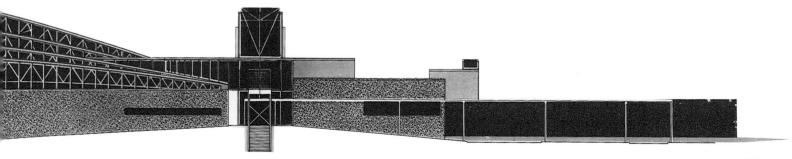

France   Renée Gailhoustet

Biography
Born in Algeria in 1929 and
moved to France in 1947.
Educated at the Sorbonne
and the Beaux Arts School
of Architecture,Paris.
Renée Gailhoustet runs her
own practice in Ivry-sur-
Seine, a suburb of Paris,
employing up to six
architects in her studio.
She has lectured at schools
of architecture in Paris,
Grenoble, and Montpelier,
France, and Sofia, Bulgaria.
She is a Professor at the
International Academy of
Archiecture, Sofia.
Selected Work:
Social housing and
community development at
Ivry-sur-Seine town centre
comprising a total of 800
apartments and
maisonettes, many with
large garden terraces. The
development also includes
shops, nursery, medical
centre, library and
workshops.In collaboration
with Jean Renaudie, 1968-
87. 700 apartments at La
Maladrerie in Aubervilliers,
France. 40 workshops, a
community centre, facilities
for the elderly and shops
are also included, 1975-86.
180 balcony apartments at
Saint Denis, France, 1987.
Apartments in Romaineville,
Villejuif and Gentilly in the
Paris suburbs, 1989.
Development on Ile de la
Reunion, Indian Ocean,
including schools,shopping
centre and a housing
cluster on a steeply sloping
site, 1986-89. Proposals for
2000 apartments in
Zaporojie, Ukraine, in
collaboration with an
international team of
architects, 1989.
Awards:
First prize in a competition
for an 800 pupil senior
school,1989. Renée
Gailhoustet's work has
been exhibited at schools of
architecture in Paris and at
the Fifth World Biennale of
Architecture, INTERARCH
89, Sofia, Bulgaria.

Renée Gailhoustet describes herself as an 'urban architect', and the title is an apt one. Since the late sevemties she has concerned herself with the problems of how to house large numbers of people in the centre of cities and how to relate housing to other parts of the city such as shops, cinemas, cafes and community services.

She writes,'For ten years the core of my work has revolved around two themes. The first is housing, more specifically what to do about social housing in this period of financial stringency and how to create living spaces which are inventive and pleasant to be in.'

'We must learn how to bring natural things back into the centre of towns. With planted balconies one can note the seasons as they pass, and courtyards let the changing sky into the centre of new developments.'

'The second theme concerns diversity in an urban context. People should not be piled up in towers or locked away on housing estates but allowed to be in the centre of the city in the midst of a great variety of buildings of differing use. That means overcoming zoning rules and endless regulations. For a while we were able to follow these difficult aims, but in France we have run into a period when discussion and development in the urban housing field is restricted. Housing is regarded purely as an economic unit, a simple piece of merchandise. 'We cannot, as architects, go on working in this superficial manner in the future and we must continue to fight against constraints which strangle invention. Otherwise we will become decorators (of whatever skill) of well targeted products.'

'This has affected my practice. I still work on interesting projects but less on social housing. The problems facing architects are not declining and excitement can always be found somewhere. But one point has nevertheless become lost, and that is the power of architects, through asking the difficult questions, to transform into active and willing citizens the lives of those who perhaps are forced to live in cities.'

Renée Gailhoustet.

Cultural Centre at Aubervilliers.

180 apartments above a shopping centre at St Denis.

41

Sweden

Kerstin Gasste

Biography
Born in Hudiksvall,
Sweden, in 1928. Educated
at the Royal Institute of
Technology, Stockholm,
completing training as an
architect in 1952.
Kerstin Gasste has
designed housing for HBS
Riksforbund, Stockholm,
since 1953. In 1954, at the
age of twenty-five, she was
made chief architect of a
group responsible for large
scale housing schemes and
was responsible for the
development of community
provision. In 1979 she
started her own practice
working full time for the
housing association HSB as
a consultant architect.
Selected Work:
Single storey houses, 42
dwellings, Orebro, 1957.
Eight storey apartment
blocks, 150 dwellings, at
Hudiksvall, 1962. Ten
storey apartment blocks,
423 dwellings, at Solna,
1965-7. Terraced houses,
21 dwellings, at
Falkenberg, 1975-6. Two
storey houses, 43
dwellings, at Falun, 1975.
Two and three storey
houses, 36 dwellings,
Landskrona, 1977. Six
storey apartment blocks, 80
dwellings, Backby,
Vasteras,1977-8.
Awards:
Prize for Church in
Skoghall, 1952. Prize for
house in Lerum, 1955.
Four prizes for holiday
houses, 1961 and 1965.
First prize for a parish hall,
Fagersta, 1976. Honour
award for old people's
housing, Kofoten,
Stockholm, Sweden, 1977.
Award for *Living in the
eighties* design competition,
Gavle, 1979.

Kerstin Gasste has worked for HSB Riksforbund, one of Sweden's large national housing associations, for nearly forty years. She joined the association, which was founded in 1930 and has housed half a million people, in 1953 when it constructed approximately eight thousand dwellings. She saw it grow to a peak of seventeen thousand dwellings per year in 1965. Today HSB provides about six and a half thousand apartments and houses each year for its co-operative tenants, community trusts and owner occupiers.

Gasste believes that architecture should reflect what is happening in society. She has fought for, and brought about, changes in housing provision.

She comments, 'In Sweden eighty per cent of women work outside the home and forty per cent of parents bring up children on their own. These facts should influence our work as architects but they are not discussed in architectural journals, it is as if we were blind. It is a pure mystery to me that journals all over the world discuss post modernism and other styles in theoretical and detached terms as if they have not noticed the revolution in mankind's life.'

'I have tried to talk about these matters in my little corner. It is a new way of life which affects the house or apartment as well as the organisation of business and industry and culture. Am I wrong? I don't think so !'

'It took me twenty-five years before I was able to convince HSB that we must try to build dwellings where people work together,have fun together and own property together - collective housing. The schemes are not big, between twenty and fifty dwellings. Every apartment is about ten square metres smaller than normal and this saved space is used for communal purposes - a big kitchen and dining room, music and film room, a hall for play and gymnastics and rooms for hobbies and a sauna. If you have twenty-five households you can have about two hundred and fifty square metres of communal space and still keep to the basic rent.'

'It is very encouraging to visit these households. People seem to like each other, children have a wonderful time and once every fourteenth day you work in the kitchen for three hours.Every other day you come down to your dining room after work and have a relaxing evening with family and friends.Of course you don't have(itals) to eat with the others. Your apartment has a complete kitchen, and on Sundays most people prefer to cook for themselves because they enjoy it.'

'There is a small kindergarten, and it must be a great advantage for children nowadays to see that there are alternative ways of living and that there are grown ups other

Kerstin Gasste

than your parents to talk to. I still remember how I used to dash to the kindergarten after work anxious not to be the last. Then to the store, and finally, feeling tired and hectic, home to cook and play with my son. I used to dream and sketch ideas for collective houses !'

'Two of my largest projects are just completed. One has three hundred and sixty dwellings, the other two hundred. Both are interesting socially as each has a collective house for twenty to thirty young households and a similar provision for older people who have similar needs. There are of course kindergartens, assembly halls and other shared places.'

Right: Timber houses in Falun, painted a deep red to match their historic neighbours, 1975.

USA Frances Halsband

Biography
Born in New York in 1943.
Won a National Merit
scholarship in 1961 and
obtained a Bachelor of Arts
degree from Swarthmore
College, Pennsylvania in
1965. In 1968 she
completed her Master of
Architecture degree from
Columbia University
Graduate School of
Architecture, New York,
and in the same year was
awarded an American
Institute of Architects
Certificate of Merit and the
William Kinne Fellowship at
Columbia University.
Fellow of the American
Institute of Architects.
From 1971 onwards she
registered as an architect
with the States of New
York, Massachusetts,
Connecticut, Pennsylvania,
Ohio, Virginia, District of
Columbia, North Carolina,
New Jersey, and New
Hampshire. She also holds
the National Council of
Architectural Registration
Boards certificate.
Partner in the firm of R.M.
Kliment and then R.M.
Kliment & Frances
Halsband Architects, New
York from 1972. The work
of the practice is varied and
ranges from sophisticated
office interiors for large
corporations in New York
and Washington, D.C., to
bold additions to university
buildings, museums, and
individual houses. The
Practice is renowned for
the great attention it pays
to detail. From 1968-72
Frances Halsband worked
for Mitchell/Giurgola
Associates Architects, New
York. From 1979 she
lectured and was a design
critic at many prestigious
schools of architecture and
at the Smithsonian
Institution in Washington,
D.C.
Selected Work:
Sixteen offices, mainly in
New York, many for
lawyers and financiers
between 1975-1989. Fifteen
individual houses,
apartments or additions

Frances Halsband, a partner in R.M. Kliment and Halsband, New York, stresses that all her work is undertaken in collaboration with her partner, R.M.Kliment.

She writes lucidly about her approach to architecture: 'In the development of our work our primary intentions are the architectural and functional integration of new buildings into existing context; the establishment of a clear calm sense of order which accomodates the function and the spirit of the use for which the building is intended; the careful making of each element, the appropriate relationship of part to part, and of each part to the new and pre-existing whole. Increasingly we look to the natural and man-made landscape as well as to the cultural context for sources of form.'

'I believe that in the next decade the theory of place, an understanding of history and appreciation of craft, and an awareness of civic responsibility will shape our work.'

'Our work includes buildings for universities, building and planning projects in civic contexts, renovation and additions to historic sites and buildings, country houses, interiors and the design of furniture and lighting.'

'I have had other opportunities to participate as an architect outside our firm. As President of the Architectural League of New York I organized exhibitions and discussions on issues that seemed relevant. "The Chair Fair" was an open competition and exhibition of chairs designed in the last ten years. The Cold Spring conferences on landscape and architecture and the exhibition "The Inhabited

Landscape" are the start of an exploration into new sources for landscape and architectural form, and for a new direction for both. These represent a different kind of collaboration from that found in an office.'

'Questioning has also been possible in my teaching, jurying and participation in public discussion, and I have taken an active role in trying to shape public policy as a Landmark Preservation Commissioner in New York City.'

44

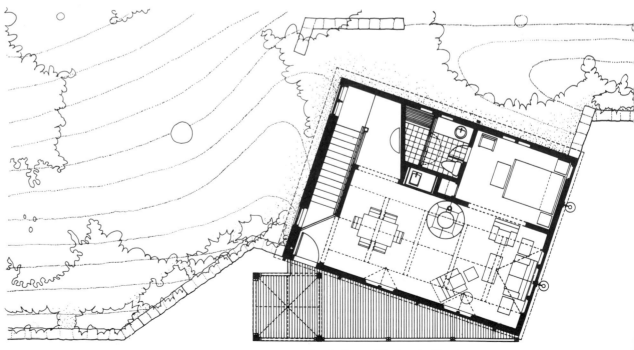

Studio House, Woodstock. Site plan.

between 1972-1988. Three museum extensions and shops in the ten years from 1973-1983. Urban design master plans for Woodstock, New York, Pasadena, California, and Margaretville and Arkville, New York between 1974-1988. Two historic renovations of large properties in New York, 1984-88. Alvin Ailey dance foundation building, New York, 1989. Three science buildings for the universities of Columbia, Virginia and Princeton, 1981-89. Town hall for Salisbury, Connecticut, 1985-8. In addition to design work with her practice she lectured between 1979 and 1988 at Harvard University, the University of California at Los Angeles and Berkeley, Tulane University, Temple University, Cranbrook Academy of Fine Art, at the Smithsonian Institution in Washington, D.C., and in Pittsburgh and Oslo, Norway. She has also been a design critic at Harvard, Columbia, and Rice Universities,as well as at the Universities of Pennsylvania, North Carolina, and the University of Virginia. In 1985 she was elected President of the Architectural League of New York, the first woman architect to hold this position. From 1984-7 she was a commissioner with the New York City Landmarks Preservation Commission and has sat on numerous architectural advisory panels as well as acting as juror on a large number of A.I.A. award committes since 1980. The firm's work has featured in 26 exhibitions between 1974 and 1989 and in more than eighty publications.
Awards:
American Bar Association large law firm award for McCarter & English law offices, New York, 1989. Bard award for Mercantile Exchange building, New York, 1989. *Progressive Architecture* citation for a Museum extension for Woodstock Artists'

Above & left: Computer Science Building, Columbia University, New York, 1983.

Association, 1974. Selected Competitor for the Women's Hall of Fame, Seneca Falls, New York, 1975. Tucker Architectural Award from the Building Stone Institute for the Computer Science Building at Columbia University, New York, 1984. *Record House* and the American Wood Council Awards for a house at Westchester County, New York, 1985. Merit Award from the Red Cedar Shingle Bureau for a studio house at Woodstock, New York, 1987. American Institute of Architects (A.I.A.) Honor Award for the Computer Science Building at Columbia University, New York, 1987.

New York City Chapter of the A.I.A. Awards: Design excellence Award for the Epstein house. Residential Design Award for Frank.S.Hogan Hall at Columbia University, New York, 1979. Residential Design Award for a country house, 1981. Distinguished Architecture Award for the Computer Science Building, Columbia University, New York, 1985. Distinguished Architecture citation for the studio house at Woodstock, New York, 1987. New York State Association of Architects awards: Design Award for a Co-operative Appartment, 1982. Design Excellence Award for Computer Science Building, Columbia University, New York, 1985.

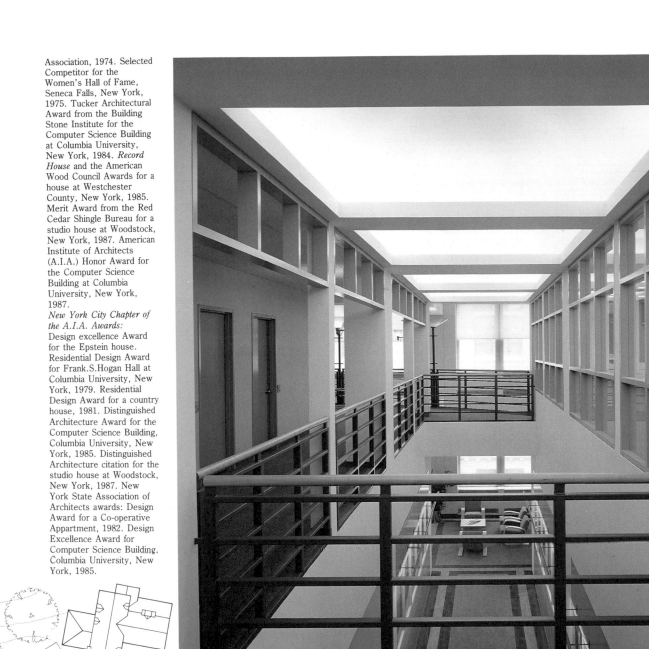

Long Island House, Remsenberg, New York State, 1987.

Advertising Offices for Levine, Huntley, Schmidt & Beaver, New York, 1989.

Studio House,
Woodstock, New York
State, 1986.

Levine, Huntley, Schmidt & Beaver,
New York, 1989. Interior Light fittings.

Long Island House,
Remsenberg. Interior.

47

Japan　　Itsuko Hasegawa

Biography
Born in Yaizu City, Japan, in 1941. Educated at the Department of Architecture, Kanto Gakuin University graduating in 1964.
Itsuko Hasegawa is principal of her own design studio in Tokyo, which she established as Itsuko Hasegawa Architectural Design Studio in 1976. The name was changed to the Architectural Design Studio in 1979. From 1964-9 she worked in Kiyonori Kikutake's office and then spent two years as a research student in the Architecture Department at Tokyo Institute of Technology. From 1971-8 she worked in Kazuo Shinohara's atelier at the Tokyo Institute of Technology. She lectured in Rotterdam, Australia, Norway and Los Angeles between 1984-7.
Selected Work:
House 1 in Yaizu, Shizuoka, 1972. House in Kamoi, Kanagawa, 1975. House in Midorigaoku, Tokyo, 1975. House 2 in Yaizu, Shizuaka, 1977. House in Kakio, Tokyo, 1977. Stationery shop in Yaizu, Shizuoka, 1978. Tokumaru children's clinic, Ehime, 1979. House in Kuwabara, Ehime, 1980. Aono building, Ehime, 1982. House in Itami, Osaka, 1982. House in Kanazamabunko, Kanagawa, 1983. NC house, Tokyo, 1984. Bizan Hall, Shizuoka, 1984. House in Ikebukoro, Tokyo, 1984. House in Oyama, Togichi, 1985. BY house, Tokyo, 1985. House in Kunamoto, 1986. House in Nerima, Tokyo, 1986. Atelier in Tomigya, Tokyo, 1986. Sugai Internal Clinic, Ehime, 1986. House in Higashi-Tamagawa, Tokyo, 1986. KK house Tokyo, 1987. Shonandai Cultural Centre, 1987-.
Awards:
First prize in open competition for the Shonandai Cultural Centre, Kanegaw, 1987.

In 1987 Itsuko Hasegawa won first prize in a competition for a cultural and community centre in Fujisawa, a city south of Tokyo. The centre, known as the Shonandai Cultural Centre, was a surprise winner and not initially popular with local residents, who had reservations about Hasegawa's plan to bury the main buildings below ground level. However, after lengthy discussions Hasegawa won round local opposition and on opening day of the first phase, in late 1989, the building met with unanimous approval. The second, and final, phase was scheduled for completion in late 1990.

Hasegawa writes forthrightly about the difficult transposition from competition project to completed scheme, and of her very Japanese approach to design.

'In Japan the light, the wind and even the air changes with the seasons, and it has been my objective to create spaces that enable one to co-exist with nature.'

'For several years my practice has been based on the concept of architecture as an interpretation of nature, instead of thinking of it as something totally based on reason and rationality.'

'The Shonandai Cultural Centre is a combination of children's pavilion, community centre and public theatre. Public buildings hitherto have tended to be very formal and I had been thinking even before the competition that such buildings ought to encourage people to drop in casually. Right after I was formally commissioned to design the centre I was given the opportunity, much to my surprise, of having direct contact with the citizens of Fujisawa - mainly because many of them objected to my creating an underground building.'

'During these discussions, which lasted up to completion of the design, I was repeatedly struck by the difficulty of designing a sufficiently complex building to accomodate a vast range of views. I made the competition entry less assertive and it was transformed into a stage set for the community.'

'First I buried underground that part of the building which would have been too conspicuous - the total volume of the building is large for the site area. I wanted to make the above ground portion a man-made park and enable everyone to use it, not just those with a special reason for coming to the centre. The plaza is a man-made garden with a stream, a pond, greenery and shelters. A path allows visitors to stroll through a roof garden and past a cluster of roofs which suggest mountains or rocks. The spheres suggest the roundness of the world, the cosmos or the moon, and there is a tower of light, wind and sound and a clock-tree along the path. The underground rooms face a sunken garden full of greenery and with walls plastered to suggest the strata through a section of earth.'

'On opening day a number of people came up to me and said that they agreed with my view that the site should be covered with two hundred varieties of plants so that it would be like a giant Ikebana reflecting the changing seasons. So the scheme is acting as a landmark in promoting environmental improvements in the surrounding area.'

In the summer of 1989 Hasegawa's design for a 270 seat theatre for the Nagoya Design exhibition was completed. Although the building was a temporary structure, built solely for the four month duration of the exhibition, she applied the same determination to interpret nature through her architecture in its design.

The exterior is made up of semi-transparent layers of perforated metal screens which reflect the sky, and blur the outline of the main building. Hasegawa refers to the visitor internally ascending 'through a space that seems enveloped in clouds and trees encountering light and wind that emphasize the materials employed.'

Palm trees, lotuses, and a high mountain are all made of fibreglass reinforced plastic or sheet metals, and the pebbles, marbles or sea shells embedded into the floor are meant to suggest a 'beach of white sand'.

Left below: Shonandai Cultural Centre, Fujisawa City, 1988-9. West Elevation

Architectural Institute of Japan award, 1986. Japan Cultural Design Award, 1986. Exhibitions in London, 1978, Paris, 1982, Moscow, 1983, and Rotterdam, 1984. Itsuko Hasegawa's work has featured in a number of international magazines and publications including *The Complete Works of Itsuko Hasegawa*, 1985.

Shonandai Cultural Centre. Man made park with stream.

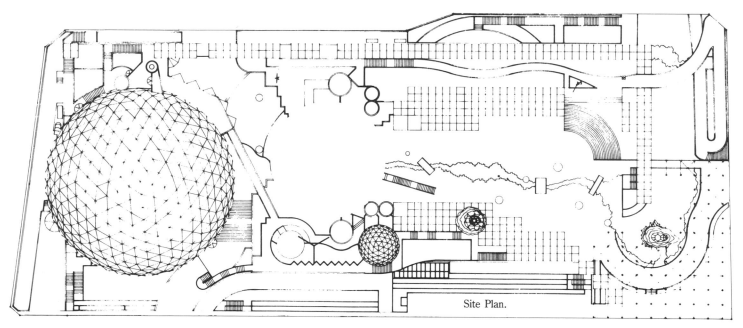

Site Plan.

Nagoya Design Expo.
Screens by day.

Shonandai Cultural
Centre. Exhibition
space.

50

Nagoya Design Expo, 1989. Perforated steel screens at night.

Shonandai Cultural Centre First Floor Plan.

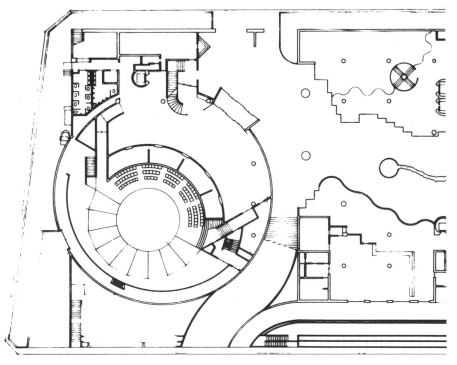

Shonandai Cultural Centre.
View of the centre as part of the city.

Sweden   Elizabeth Hatz

Biography
Born in Lund, Sweden in 1953.
Educated at the Architectural Association, London, 1972-77. Member of Berg Arkitektkontor, Stockholm, since 1979. Prior to joining Berg, Elizabteh Hatz worked for a two year period in Paris undertaking projects as varied as a school for handicapped children, the interior of a Senegalese palace, a Parisian restaurant, a fountain at Cergy Pontoise and on the final stage of a competition for a foodmarket at St Quentin.
Selected work with Berg:
Head offices and laboratories for Kodak, Gothenburg,1979-82. Offices for the teachers trade union, Stockholm, 1982-84, in conjunction with Maud Vretblad. Research laboratory/greenhouse with study rooms and library, Stockholm, 1985-6. Stockholm Globe arena, the world's largest spherical building, containing a main 16,000 seat arena, training arena, offices, hotel, restaurants etc., 1986-89, in conjunction with a five person design team from Berg. Administration office pavilion at the Globe, 1988-89. Ms Hatz taught at the Royal Technical High School school of architecture, Stockholm from 1983-6 and sits on the board of the National Swedish Board of Architects, SAR. In 1987 she was elected to the board of ATHENA, the Swedish Women Architects Association.

Elizabeth Hatz joined Berg Architektkontor, a large Swedish practice based in Stockholm, in 1979. The projects she has undertaken with the firm have grown in size and prestige as the years have passed, culminating in her becoming a leading member of the design team to complete the world's largest spherical building - a sports arena called 'The Globe' in Stockholm, finished amidst much acclaim in 1989.

Like many of her colleagues in Scandinavia, where natural light is in short supply for many months of the year, she is aware of the psychological effect this has upon people and the designer's need to use available light in creative ways.

'Architecture has to do with a sense of place and a sense of presence', she states. 'This, together with its ability to spread and divide light, is perhaps the most fundamental but least explainable impact it has on us.'

In looking for a 'sense of place and presence' in architecture she is searching for a timelessness in the buildings she designs which will serve the needs of future generations as well as the present. She continues, 'I wish to discover what makes some places and buildings more congenial than

The Triangle at the Globe. This pavilion on stilts is administration offices and a meeting point for those queuing for last minute tickets.

Left below: The Globe, Stockholm, 1989. This 16,000 seat arena for sports and cultural events lies to the south of the city centre. It incorporates 5 office buildings, a shopping centre and an hotel in addition to sports training and main arenas.

The Globe stamps, 1989.

others -not as objects or sculptures but as places to be in and as the background for people's lives. The timelessness of architecture lies in its ability to offer infinite variety of use in the years to come for people whose needs are as yet unspecified.'

In approaching a new project Elizabeth Hatz is loath to commit herself to put pen to paper, seeking a long period of rumination beforehand.

'Each new architectural task generates a mixture of joy and fear - a state of internal chaos where gradually a whirl of impressions from within and without gather together. This process may give an indication of the character of the future scheme. Even if this chaos gives you the feeling of starting from zero each time, it may be a fruitful way of allowing

53

Kodak Headquarters and laboratories, Gothenburg, 1982.

new dimensions to emerge before having to whip them into shape in a design. I postpone sketching for as long as possible and then, when I do start, the first sketches never manage to record the complete vision of what I am looking for, but they remain important throughout the rest of the work. I would not say this was a work method, rather an approach to each job which has something in common.'

Keno Gard, research laboratory, Stockholm, 1986.

Keno Gard, research laboratory. Interior.

Britain   # Christine Hawley

Biography
Born in Shrewsbury in
1949. Educated at the
Architectural Association
School of Architecture
London, 1969-75, obtaining
the A.A. Diploma in 1975.
Registered with the
Architect's Registration
Council for the United
Kingdom (A.R.C.U.K),
1978, member of the Royal
Institute of British
Architects (R.I.B.A.),
1982, and Fellow of the
Royal Society of Arts
(F.R.S.A.), 1983. She has
received three British
Council awards, one in
1977, two in 1979.
Christine Hawley is
principal in the firm Cook
and Hawley in London. In
partnership with Peter
Cook she has won prizes
for five international
competitions entries in a
nine year period. She is
also head of the
Department of Architecture
at the Polytechnic of East
London, 1988-, and has
taught in the United States,
Norway and West
Germany. From 1975-7 she
worked for the De Soissons
Partnership in London,
followed by a short period
with Yorke Rosenberg and
Mardell (Y.R.M.) and
Pearson International
Architects, 1977-8.
Teaching: Chelsea School of
Art, London, 1976-7,
Architectural Association
School of Architecture,
London, 1978-, Staatlisches
Hochschüle für Bildende
Kunst, Frankfurt, 1979-,
and Acting Head of
Department, 1980-1,
Arkitekturhogskule, Oslo,
1982, Carnegie Mellon
University, Pittsburgh,
1982, North East London
Polytechnic, 1982- and
Head of Diploma
Department since 1984,
Head of Department,
1988-. Visiting Professor at
Western Australia Institute
of Technology, Perth,
1985, Hyde Professor at
Lincoln University,
Nebraska, 1987, Visiting
Professor at Oslo School of

Christine Hawley and Peter Cook have progressed from the visionary work of Archigram, a group of influential teachers at the Architectural Association in the sixties and early seventies, who saw tremendous excitement in the possibilities offered by high technology and dense urban development. With the formation of Cook and Hawley in 1974, both previous members of Archigram developed their work through competition entries into more buildable forms. It was now possible to see that they were not only inspiring teachers and theorists but also capable of designing constructable buildings.

Christine Hawley has managed to balance teaching and design careers. In 1988 she was appointed Head of the Department of Architecture at the North East London Polytechnic after a four year period as Head of the Diploma Department during which she successfully fought a number of battles on the school's behalf with the R.I.B.A and the Council for National Academic Awards. Her school offers 'day release' programmes for those wishing to become qualified architects while employed, and this has opened up architectural studies to students who would otherwise be unable to commit themselves financially to a seven year course.

Cook and Hawley completed two small buildings in the late eighties and early nineties. In Japan two exhibition structures in Nagoya and Osaka were constructed for Textile and Design Exhibitions, but their chance to build on a larger scale had started its long gestation period many years before.

In the 1980s they were asked to design a museum for stained glass at Langen in Hesse and produced an exciting and uncompromisingly modern proposal. The scheme was not well received by local planning authorities due to the sensitivity of the site in a part of the historic old town, and endless delays occurred. In 1989 it was unclear whether the scheme will ever be built.

In 1984 Hawley and Cook were asked, at the personal invitation of the Director of the Internationale Bau Austellung (I.B.A.), to design housing and shops in Lutzowplatz in West Berlin. Here was their first chance to prove their worth on a prestigious site and in the company of other notable architects - a scheme by Mario Botta is attached to their design. Delays occurred with the Berlin planning authorities but the I.B.A., to its credit, stuck with its plans, and the building was finally completed in mid 1990 - six years later.

Housing for the I.B.A., Lutzowplatz, West Berlin, 1984-90. Front Elevation.

Architecture, 1988. Visiting critic at the Bartlett School of Architecture, University College, London, 1986 and external examiner, 1988. Visiting critic at the Southern California Institute of Technology, 1987.

Selected work:
Three houses in London. Solar Houses in Landstuhl, West Germany. Antique Exchange shop, London. Apartments and shops for Internationale Bau Ausstellung (I.B.A.), West Berlin, 1984-90. Kindergarten, Sachsenhausen, Frankfurt. Stained Glass Museum, Langen, Hesse. Exhibition pavilion, Nagoya, 1989, Japan. Exhibition pavilion, Osaka, 1990, Japan. Speculative houses, Kuala Lumpur, Malaysia. Proposals for extension for the Stadelschule Museum, Frankfurt. Proposals for over 50s work/residential development, Dundee, Scotland.

Awards:
Second prize (500 entries) Shinkenchiku Housing competition, Tokyo, 1976. Project selected for RIBA/ Building Design competition, 1977. Yamagiwa Art Foundation Award, Tokyo, 1979. Fifth prize, DOM office competition building, Bruhl, West Germany, 1980. First prize, Karmeliter Museum, Frankfurt, 1981. First prize for solar housing competition, Landstuhl, West Germany, 1982. First prize for a sports hall competition, Hoechst, Frankfurt, 1985. Second prize for Hamburg Millentor area development study, 1985. Cook and Hawley's work has been published in thirty eight publications between 1977-89 in England, West Germany, France, the United States, Japan, Norway and Italy. Drawings of their projects are in eleven private and public collections and their work has featured in thirty one exhibitions from 1976-1989.

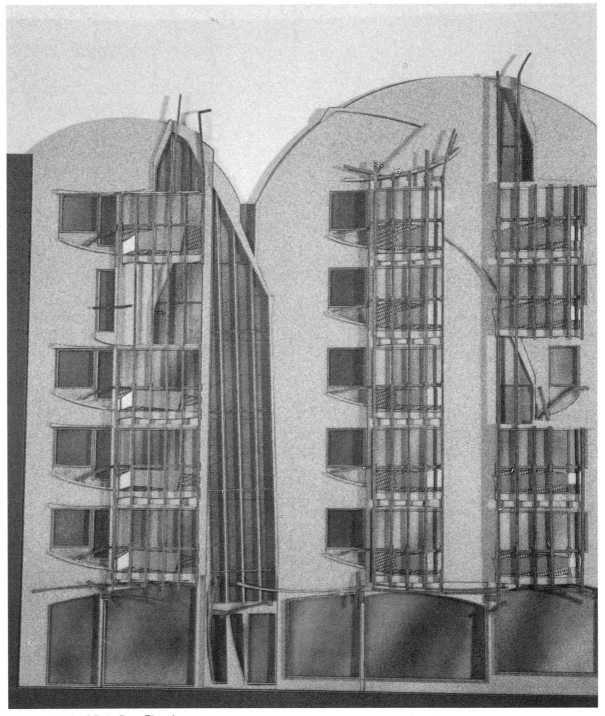

Housing for the I.B.A. Rear Elevation.

Nigeria   Gillian Hopwood

Gillian Hopwood

Biography
Born in Britain in 1927.
Educated at the
Architectural Association
School of Architecture,
London, 1945-50,
Architectural Association
Diploma, 1950. First
woman to be made a
Fellow of the Nigerian
Institute of Architects,
1983. Fellow of the Royal
Institute of British
Architects. Member of the
Corona Schools Trust
Council, 1970-. First Vice
President of Soroptimist
International of Nigeria,
1989-90.
Gillian Hopwood is
Executive Director and
Company Secretary of
Godwin Hopwood Kuye,
Lagos, Nigeria, and an
Associate of Frank Mbanefo
Associates, Enugu, and
Godwin and Hopwood,
London. She has lived and
worked in Nigeria since
1955 where she has
worked closely with her
husband John Godwin.
Selected work:
Five multi-storey low cost
primary schools for the
Ministry of Education,
Lagos, 1955-63. Boarding
School for the Deaf and
Day School for the Blind,
1958-60. School classroom,
laboratories and hall used
as student accomodation for
the University of Lagos,
1960. Private houses and
office extensions, 1955-60.
Federal Science School
funded by the World Bank
and Ministry of Education,
Lagos, 1960-71. Multi

Gillian Hopwood and John Godwin opened their practice in Lagos in 1955 and worked in Nigeria through the boom years of the 1960s and 1970s. Thirty four years later they amalgamated the practice with Tunde Kuye Associates to form Godwin Hopwood Kuye. A London practice was opened in 1987, under the name Godwin Hopwood, and both offices serve the needs of their multi-national industrial clients.

Commissions have covered a wide range of buildings but the practice has become best known for its educational and industrial work in Nigeria. It offers a range of consultancy services which have varied from participation in the General Electric Company's design team for a country wide telecommunications system to taking the leading role in the planning, design, construction and management of a new town outside Lagos called Agbara Estate.

'I do not believe in architecture with a capital A,' states Gillian Hopwood. 'All buildings are a compromise; an amalgam of what the client thinks is needed, interpretation of the brief in architectural terms tempered by cost restrictions, and the ability of the building industry.'

'Building in Nigeria has been exciting. Maxwell Fry and Jane Drew had studied the requirements of the tropics and were completing the first phase of the University of Ibadan in 1954. We followed on, looking at the effects of orientation, through-ventilation, sunshading and the separate requirements of the broad climatic zones of the country. The building industry was dominated by Italians who have made an enormous contribution to the development of the labour force by teaching tradesmen. On site their efforts were directed towards getting the building well built and teamwork was the order of the day. This state of affairs has continued, though in the present harsh economic climate it becomes more and more difficult to achieve.'

Despite the decline of rapid growth in Nigeria in the late 1980s Godwin Hopwood have an impressive list of projects on hand: two offices for Shell Petroleum and Texaco Nigeria, seven housing projects including staff accomodation for Gulf Oil and Metal Box Nigeria, three brewery extensions for Guinness, plus four more industrial projects, seven educational buildings, an eye hospital, a yacht club and a High Court complex.

storey office building, Lagos, 1966. Philips Radio and Philite factory, Lagos, 1966. Apartments, service buildings and servants quarters for Shell Petroleum, Lagos, 1967-70. Branch bank and Area office for United Bank of Africa, Benin, 1970-1. Can factory for Metal Box of Nigeria, Lagos, 1971. Bookshop House, a commercial development for the Church Missionary Society, Lagos, 1977-8. Standard design for a single storey house which was built in Jos, Plateau state, Kano, Kano State and Kaduna, Kaduna State, 1978-9. Senior Staff Club design, Ogunu, Bendel State, 1980. Standard design for a block of six or eight apartments built for Costain Nigeria Ltd., Lagos, 1980-1. Apartments, service buildings and servants quarters for Leventis Nigeria Ltd., Ikoyi, 1981-3. 1983- 9. Office and apartment refurbishments. Houses on Victoria Island, Lagos, and in Benin. Alterations to form a maternity Hospital, Ikoyi. Alterations to three houses in Britain. Gillian Hopwood and John Godwin have written a history of the Lagos Yacht Club, 1982 and have a book about Lagos buildings in preparation. They have always been conscious of their duty to train members of their staff and fourteen Nigerian practices are now headed by ex-members of staff.

Left: Christchurch Cathedral Primary School, Lagos, c 1960.
Above: Apartments for Lewventis Ltd., Ikoyi, Lagos, 1981-3.
Right: Standard Apartments for Costain Nigeria, 1980-1.

Holland   Francine Houben

Biography
Born in Sittard, 1955.
Educated at the
Department of
Architecture, Technical
University, Delft,
graduating in 1984.
Francine Houben is one of
five partners of Mecanoo
Architekten a practice
started in Delft in 1981 as
a result of a competition
victory. Mecanoo's chief
interest lies in improving
the quality of housing
design. Houben has been a
guest teacher at the
Adamsee School, 1987-8,
and is a member of the 5x5
pressure group. She has
been a jury member for the
following awards; Ikitnos
award, Rotterdam, 1985,
Youth Hostel, Delft, 1985,
Premidee, Groningen,
1986, and the Dutch
European competition,
1988. She has lectured in
West Germany and Belgium
and at the Universities of
Delft, Amsterdam,
Eindhoven and Rotterdam.
Selected work:
Student accomodation in
Bedrijfsruimten Kruisplein,
Rotterdam, 1980-5.
Caminada dwellings, Delft,
1984-7. Bospolder-
Tussendijken dwellings,
Rotterdam, 1984-7.
'Hillekop' dwellings,
Bedrijfsruimten
Afrikaanderwijk, Rotterdam,
1985-8. Apartments,
Bedrijfsruimten Tiendplein,
Rotterdam, 1985-. Fruit
Farm, Wilhelminadorp,
1986-8. Miller's Barbershop
interior, The Hague, 1987.
Villa Huntum, Amsterdam,
1986-. Apartments in
Winkels Gerard Dubuurt,
Amsterdam, 1986.
Apartments in Groningen,
1986-. Gallery Bebert,
Rotterdam. Botanical
Laboratory, Wageningen,
1986-. Apartments in
Katendrecht, Rotterdam,
1986-. Dapperburt urban
planning project,
Amsterdam, 1987. Urban
plan, 1000 dwellings, for
former market, the Hague,
1989-.

Francine Houben is a member of the Delft-based practice Mecanoo. As a student at the Technical University, she and four other students, now partners with her, entered a competition for student housing in Rotterdam. When they won, and were commissioned to build their design, the practice was formed.

Mecanoo's logo - a sky diver, arms stretched wide in mid-jump - is supremely appropriate for a company which started with one project and no idea where it might lead. As time has passed this leap into the unknown has brought many challenges and many rewards.

In 1987 they were awarded the Rotterdam-Maaskant award for young architects - their fifth major award in seven years - and promptly took on a quarter of Rotterdam's public housing quota.

Francine Houben has a strongly felt commitment to improve the quality of Dutch housing and public spaces. She admires the aims of the Modern Movement with its desire to challenge the status quo, and started the 5x5 working party, a group of architects, politicians and housing corporation representatives and residents to raise the level of debate in Holland. The group issued a manifesto, in the form of a poster calling for a stop to the lack of care paid to housing issues in Holland in the hope that all interested parties would unite to improve matters. Time will tell, but Mecanoo will continue to press for the right to be allowed to develop its own theories and put them into practice.

As the group's reputation has grown so too has its list of clients. The majority of its work is housing. Its 1985 design for apartments in Rotterdam, known as the Hillekop scheme, comprises two strongly contrasting elements; a sixteen storey fan shaped tower and a six storey block which boldly snakes its way over Rotterdam's railway lines.

In 1986 the practice was asked to design a fruit farm research station for the Dutch Ministry of Agriculture in Zeeland. It was completed in 1987 and proudly stands, a silver shed with round eyes and an undulating roof, amidst the surrounding fruit fields. Although quite unlike traditional farm buildings found elsewhere in the region, it proves a satisfying and unusual addition to the landscape.

Fruit Farm Research Station, Wilhelminadorp, 1986-8.

Awards:
First Prize, student
accomodation in Rotterdam
competition, 1980. First
Prize, UNESCO
'Tomorrow's Habitat'
competition, 1984. First
Prize, Housing in Delft
competition, 1984. First
Prize, Housing in
Groningen, 1985. Awarded
the Rotterdam-Maaskant
prize for young architects,
1987.

Hillekop housing
development in South
Rotterdam, 1985-8.

Proposals for housing in
Antigua, 1989.

West Germany Christine Jachmann

Christine Jachmann

Biography
Born in Lunegurg in 1949.
Educated in Dusseldorf and
Zurich, town planning
studies at the Technical
University, Berlin.
Christine Jachmann has run
her own practice in Cologne
and Berlin since 1972. She
is a member of the town
planning commission in
Berlin.
Selected work:
'Wohnanlage am Park', 234
apartments, 2 shops and a
restaurant, Berlin, 1978-80.
Roof conversions, Berlin,
1981. 2 multi-family
dwellings each with 8
apartments, Berlin, 1982. 1
block of 20 apartments,
Berlin, 1982. 28 apartments
and premises for a bank
and restaurant in
Wittenbergplatz, Berlin,
1984-6. Furniture, shoe
design and bank interior,
1985. Conservation and
restoration work, Berlin,
1986-9. Proposals for a
block of 120 'model
dwellings'for the
Internationale Bau
Austellung (I.B.A.), Berlin,
1988-90, in conjunction with
5 international architects.
Her work has been
exhibited in Britain, the
United States, Poland,
West Germany and France.
She has been in the film
Story of Women Architects
by H.Ortlieb.

Christine Jachmann's designs for one hundred and thirty 'model dwellings' for the Internationale Bau Austellung (I.B.A.) in Berlin stand next to those of a fellow architect from Berlin, and British, Polish and American architects.

The developer behind the I.B.A. scheme drew together designs for publicly funded housing by well known architects all over the world with the intention of building a showcase of late 1980s architecture. The plan is similar to that of the late 1920s 'Weissenhof Siedlung,' a row of exhibition houses perched on a hill overlooking Stuttgart, where contemporary architects designed single family houses suitable for modern life.

As with all idealistic proposals the world over, the I.B.A. scheme ran into bureaucratic difficulties and many of the plans may remain on the drawing board. This has not however dulled the enthusiasm of those who see a chance to improve living standards.

'Concepts of emancipated forms of living within the framework of publicly financed housing', blazons forth Christine Jachmann's *raison d'étre* for her design of apartments in I.B.A. Block 2.

She continues: 'Ways of living and living conditions have changed. Current regulations for apartment types do not leave possibilities for living differently. Everything is suited to the needs of those who have an established way of life. Subsidized apartments in new buildings can only be used by traditional families and not by people living together in freer forms or in communes.'

Living together, whether in an apartment or, until late 1989, an isolated city such as Berlin, is something to which Christine Jachmann has devoted much time and thought. It is no surprise to discover that West Berliners, who for decades had no free access to the surrounding countryside, have taken great pains to 'green' their city.

Christine Jachmann's 'Wohnanlage am Park' housing development of two hundred and thirty four apartments, 1978-80, backs directly on to a park in the Wilmersdorf area of Berlin. Even allowing for this proximity to open space Jachmann gives every tenant a large balcony, many of which are covered with flowers.

Private open space features prominently again in her 1984 design for an apartment block in Berlin's Schoneberg area, but in addition to balconies she breaks out at roof level with top floor conservatories and roof gardens.

Left below: 'Wohnen am Volkspark', Apartments, Berlin-Wilmersdorf, 1978-80.

Apartments, Volksbank and restaurant, Wittenbergplatz, Berlin, 1984-6.

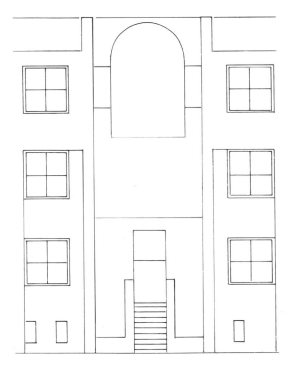

Far right: Wittenbergplatz apartments.
Right: Roof garden, Wittenbergplatz apartments.

Britain   Eva Jiricna

Biography
Born in Czechoslovakia in
1939, arrived in London,
1968. Educated at the
University of Prague School
of Architecture and Town
Planning, qualifying as an
engineer/architect in 1962.
Master of Arts degree from
the Academy of Fine Arts,
Prague, 1967. Royal
Institute of British
Architects part 3:
Professional practice and
Management, 1973.
Eva Jiricna Architects was
started in London in 1987.
The practice is known for
its sophisticated shop
interiors in which use is
made of industrial materials
and elements. The practice
was known as Jiricna Kerr
Associates from 1985-7,
and prior to this Eva Jiricna
practiced on her own from
1982-5. She was in
partnership with David
Hodge from 1980-2, and
was an associate of the De
Soisson Partnership from
1969-80. For one year after
her arrival in London in
1968 she worked for the
Greater London Council
Schools Division. She has
lectured at schools of
architecture and is a council
member of the
Architectural Association,
London.
Selected work:
1980-2: Le Caprice
Restaurant, London. Joseph
Tricot shop, London.
Chinese Laundry shop,
London. Kenzo Shop,
London. Apartments in
Chelsea and Belsize Park,
London. Apartment for
Joseph Ettedgui ('Joseph'),
London. 1982-5. All for
Joseph Ettedgui: Second
apartment, London.
L'Express cafe, London.
Pour La Maison shop,
London. Joseph Tricot,
Paris. 1985-7: Lloyds
Headquarters interiors in
collaboration with Richard
Rogers. Renovation of
Harrods' 'Way In'
department. Joseph Bis
shop, London. Joe's Cafe,
London. Joseph Pour La
Maison, London. Joseph

A number of architects resent being seen as experts in only one area so it seems somewhat ironic that Eva Jiricna, trained not as an interior designer but as an architect and engineer, is best known for her beautiful shop interiors in the smartest cities throughout the world.

Her legendary innovative work in London in the 1980s for Joseph Ettedgui, owner of the 'Joseph' shops, opened the floodgates to a torrent of retail clients all admiring her designs and hoping to reap similar financial success. Commissions flooded in for high fashion shops in London, Los Angeles, Paris, Florence, Montreal and Copenhagen.

Her engineering training shows through clearly in the minimalist design of glass and steel staircases in a number of her projects, but it is only as the 1990s progress that her consummate skill will be seen to flourish in wider fields.

Two projects for the international furnishing company, Vitra, have brought her a refreshing change - and allowed her to consider designing the *outside* of buildings. Vitra, which is based in Basle, Switzerland, commissioned Eva Jiricna Architects, to design new headquarters for it in 1988.

The scheme, though not built, shows the practice's approach. In 1989 Vitra returned for the design of a canopy, known as the 'Vitra Bridge', for its offices in Basle.

1990 brings completion of a house design in London. It involves thorough structural change and is seen by the practice as a contrast to the elegant apartment interiors which have won awards from the architectural press. But the mainstay of the practice remains the same - commercial and retail refurbishment.

below:

Vitra Headquarters, Basle, Switzerland, 1988. Model. The client wished to centralize administration and develop a future headquarters in Basle. Four individual blocks are proposed, connected at ground level, and with the possibility of a bridge at higher level. Natural light and ventilation enter central parts of the building from two vertical light wells. Structural steel supports are on the outside of the building, leaving internal space free for either open plan or cellular offices. The atrium, in the centre of the scheme, houses the canteen, exhibition space and landscaped areas.

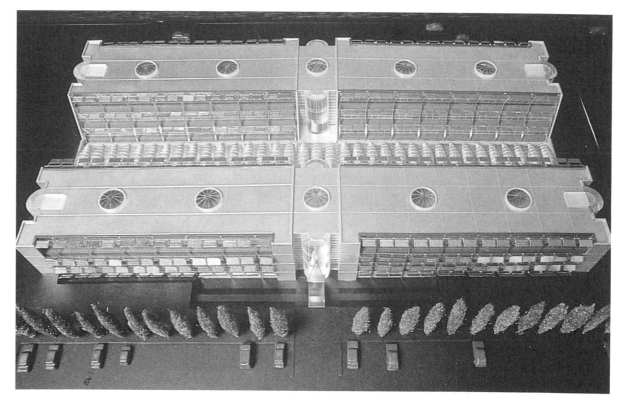

Tricot, London. Joseph Pour La Ville, London. Legends Night club and restaurant, London. Vidal Sassoon salons in London and Frankfurt. Four apartments in London. Shop at Copenhagen airport, Denmark. Retail system for Planet fashion, London. 1987-: Shops in London, Paris and Copenhagen. Shops in Los Angeles, San Francisco, Montreal, London and Paris. Boutiques in Florence and Riccione, Italy. Office for shipowners. Retail system, Switzerland. Vitra bridge canopy, Basle, Switzerland. Project for Vitra Headquarters, Basle, Switzerland. Shops for the 'Joseph' empire, London. Commercial refurbishment. London. Major changes to a private house and apartment, London.
Awards:
First prize in the Westminster Pier competition, London, 1981, (with David Hodges) Third prize for Robertson's Leisure Park, Battersea, London. First prize for Hampton site, London. Dunlopillo prize for innovation. First prize, Retail category,' Interiors' magazine, New York. ' A.D.' awards for Kenzo shop, apartment in Belsize Park and apartment for Joseph Ettedgui, 1980-2. Exhibitions: Furniture design for Formica Color-Core exhibition. Ideal Standard exhibit at the Building Centre, London.

Bridge for Vitrashop A.G, Basle, 1989. The bridge is constructed from black painted tubular steel bearing on a single central support with sandblasted glass treads and a stainless steel balustrade. The dramatic PVC cover is supported by a space truss, and anchored by cables to the ground.

Australia Louise St John Kennedy

Biography
Born in 1950. Educated at
the University of Western
Australia, Bachelor of
Science,1970 and the
University of Melbourne,
Bachelor of Architecture,
1978. Associate of the
Royal Australian Institute of
Architects (A.R.A.I.A.)
Member of the Society of
Interior Designers of
Australia.
Louise St John Kennedy is
principal in her firm, Louise
St John Kennedy &
Associates in Cottesloe,
Western Australia. The
practice designed a large
number of houses in the
early 1980s, one of which
won an award for the most
outstanding work of
domestic architecture in
Australia. Prior to starting
her own firm she worked
for Robert Cann &
Associates in Perth,
Western Australia, Gunn
Hayball Ltd.in Melbourne,
Victoria, and Cameron
Chisholm & Nichol Ltd. in
Perth, Western Australia.
She was honorary secretary
of the Western Australia
chapter of the
R.A.I.A.,1982-3 and a juror
on awards committees from
1980-8. She is the first
woman to be appointed to
the Board of the Architects
Board of Western Australia,
1984-, and has been a
registration examiner for
the board since 1984. She
is a member of the Board
of Perth Institute of
Contemporary Art, 1988-,
and was asked by the
Minister of Housing to join
the Government/Industry
committee on state and
local government land and
housing regulations, 1986.
She has spoken at
conferences at the
University of Western
Australia, 1985, and at the
Singapore conference of the
Urban Development
Institute, 1986.
Selected work:
All buildings are in Western
Australia. Ruse house,
Subiaco, 1980 Smalley
house, Dalkeith, 1981. Car

Louise St John Kennedy works on the West coast of Australia outside Perth.

It was inevitable that after winning an award for the most outstanding piece of domestic architecture in Australia in 1984 that she would be inundated with clients asking her to design houses. Those living in the well to do Perth suburbs of Claremont, Cottesloe and Subiaco flocked to her practice and she completed twenty four individual houses in an eight year period.

In 1986 there was uproar in wealthy Mosman Park when Dallas Dempster, one of the residents, asked Louise St John Kennedy to design a public tearoom jutting out into the water of Mosman Bay. After lengthy wrangles and much vociferous opposition from local residents, who saw it as a threat to the exclusivity of their area, the tearoom was built and received loud praise from the public and architectural press. Even the residents were won over by the charm of the design and revised their opinion. The tearoom's shed like shape, floating over the clear blue water of Mosman Bay, and the delicacy of its latticed wooden structure is reminiscent of traditional boathouses in the region.

Chester Road residences, Perth.

gallery workshops, Fremantle, 1981. Fenbury house, Subiaco, 1981. Downes-Stoney house,East Perth, 1983. Haywood house, Bedforddale, 1983. The Pines Business Centre, Cottesloe, 1983. Office foyesr and interior, Perth, 1983. McCarter house, Claremont, 1983. Smetana house, Cottesloe, 1984. Tannock house, Claremont, 1984. Seven houses, Claremonet, 1984. Cribb house, Cottesloe, 1985. Dempster house, Mosman Park, 1985. Hutton house, Broome, 1985. Harry house, Claremont, 1985. Tayman house, Nedlands, 1985. Mosman Bay Boatshed and Tearooms, Mosman Park, 1986. San Lorenzo restaurant, Claremont, 1987. Burt house, Quindalup, 1987. Nicholson Road offices, Subiaco, 1988. Riseley Square shopping centre, Applecross, 1988.

Awards:
Western Chapter of the R.A.I.A. Commendations for houses in Subiaco,1980, East Perth, 1984 and Claremont, Western Australia, 1987.
Architecture Design Award for housc in Dalkcith, Western Australia,1983.
Award of Specific Merit for Gallery, workshop and residence, Fremantle, Western Australia, 1983.
Robyn Boyd Award for the most outstanding Australian domestic architecture for house in East Perth, Western Australia, 1984.
Fremantle award for outstanding contribution to the built environment of the city for Gallery, workshop and residence, Fremantle, Western Australia,1983.
Her work has been the subject of twenty seven articles in periodicals between 1980-7, and has featured in two books, *Details in Australian Architecture*, R.A.I.A., 1984, and *Australian Built*, Australian Council, 1985.

Above left: Chester Road residences, Perth. Front elevation with pedimented entrance door.

Above: Interior.
Overhead light floods downwards onto the dining area.

The red swimming pool.

Property Resources
office, Subiaco, Perth.

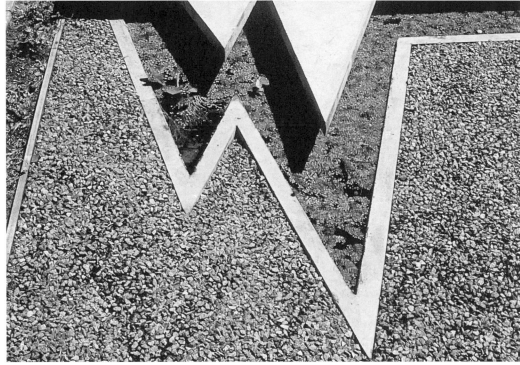

Detail of front entry path with blue pebble garden, pond and
water plants.

Rear courtyard and conference area with outdoor bar. An undulating canopy is made from corrugated iron sheeting – a gesture to a long serving Australian building material.

Left: Mosman Bay, Perth

USSR

Zoe Kharitonova, Valve Pormeister, & Natalya Zakharina

Biography
Zoe Kharitonova.
Working in Moscow.
Member of the N.E.R.
group (known as the New
Element of Settlement)
since late 1960.
Responsible, with the
group, for the development
of new approaches to
renovation and revitalization
in the historic areas of the
city.
Valve Pormeister.
Working in Tallin, Estonia.
She has worked on a
number of prestigious local
projects since the late
1950s, many of which
reflect the needs of local
farming communities.
Selected work:
Flower pavilion and cafe
'Tuljak', Tallin, 1960.
Office building for Estonian
Scientific Poultry Farms,
Kurtna, 1966. Exhibition
pavilion, Saku, 1972.
Estonian Republican Centre
of Plant Protection, Saku,
1975. Agricultural School,

The work of Zoe Kharitonova, Valve Pormeister and Natalya Zakharina from the Soviet Union is little known outside their country. This is a shameful reflection of the minimal knowledge the West has of their considerable achievements and status at home.

As Viacheslav Glazitchev of the Soviet Union of Architects writes from Moscow, 'We have the honour to present (to) you the work of Ms Zakharina, whose works and personality are most popular in the Soviet Union.'

In Estonia, Juri Jaama, President of the Union of Estonian Architects in Tallin, affirms his colleagues' regard for Valve Pormeister. 'In our opinion the works of Estonian women architects in the twentieth century have been interesting and at a high level - and Ms Pormeister is one of the best among them without doubt.'

All three architects work for the State and have been members of their local area Architects Union throughout their careers. Under Mikhail Gorbachev co-operatives have been allowed to start, and some young architects have formed their own consultancies offering design services. However, there are still difficulties with the translation from design into built form as the construction industry has many problems to sort out.

Zoe Kharitonova lives and works in Moscow. She is a member of a group of architects renowned since the late 1960s for their development of new architectural theories, known as the 'New Element of Settlement' (N.E.R.) group. The members have been very active ever since in developing concepts and projects for new Soviet approaches to the historic city: pedestrianisation, sensitive infill and intelligent rehabilitation of old nineteenth century buildings. They have generated excitement amongst their Moscow based colleagues and brought about considerable change in both attitude and practice towards urban planning and design.

Valve Pormeister was born in Tallin, Estonia, in 1922 and graduated from the University of Tartu and Tallin State Art Institute in 1952.

'By nationality I am an Estonian', she writes, 'I work in Tallin at the Estonian Project Bureau, Eesti Maehitus Project. I am a member of the Estonian Architects Union and on its ruling board. At present I am working on the designs for an exhibition and conference centre in Tallin.'

Her training as a landscape architect is reflected in her concern to relate buildings sympathetically to the land, and many of her projects have been connected to local agricultural needs. In 1966 she designed an experimental fowl

Left: Apartments in Zelenogorsk, near Leningrad, 1982-4. Natalya Zakharina.

breeding station at Kurtna; and in 1971 she was one of three architects responsible for the redevelopment of Saku, an historic village near Tallin, as a new agricultural town. It was awarded a USSR State Prize for Architecture in 1971.

In 1966 she designed an office for the Estonian Poultry Farms Centre in Kurtna and in 1975 designed highly regarded low rise, steeply pitched roof buildings on a lakeside for the Janeda State Farm Technical School. She continued building for agricultural research and training centres with the Estonian Scientific Centre for Cattle Breeding in Tartu, 1978, and the Agricultural Academy in Tartu, 1983.

The Pirita State Floricultural farm brought her the opportunity to design a cafe in 1966 and she has built two more, one in Viljandi in 1977, and in Kurtna ten years later.

Natalya Zakharina, like her colleagues, designs and builds for her local area. She lives and works in Leningrad, and her buildings are to be found there or in the nearby towns, Pushkin and Zelenogorsk. She has won a number of architectural prizes for her designs.

One award winner is her shopping and community centre, built from 1979-81 in Zelenogorsk, which sits amidst silver birch trees and an artificial lake. The clean lines of the architecture and landscaping are not cluttered with extensive car parks, as one would expect in retail developments in many other countries.

Her large scale housing development in Pushkin, 1970-

80, scooped two prizes. Four, five and ten storey apartments, many with small well planted private balconies, overlook large landscaped communal parks.

By 1984, when she completed a housing scheme in Zelenogorsk, a number of changes are noticeable. Buildings range from two to six storeys high and are brick rather than concrete or stucco. Variety is built in to the design through the clustering of low apartment blocks around small courtyards; larger individual balconies are provided for those on the third storey or higher, with planters built in to the balcony wall; hard and soft landscaped areas are well thought out, and traffic is kept well away from pedestrian areas.

Natalya Zakharina has also designed public buildings. Her 1965 design for a crematorium in Leningrad inexplicably took eighteen years to completion in 1983. Its low, Modern Movement groups of buildings are designed around a formal, central courtyard in which tall firs reach skywards. Formal landscaped areas stretch around the buildings on all sides, and wide flights of steps overlook two sombre stretches of water.

Her treatment of the Communist Party Headquarters building in Pushkin, 1979-86, shows a far less solemn approach and bobs a curtsy to Leningrad's great historic buildings. The initial design drawings in 1979 show a people's palace with courtyard fountains and formal gardens surmounted by a waving banner proudly proclaiming the client's name.

Right: Agricultural School, Janeda, Estonia, 1975. Valve Pormeister.

Austria Karla Kowalski

Biography
Born in Oberschleisen, now part of Poland, in 1941. Educated at the Technical University, Darmstadt, West Germany, and the Architectural Association School of Architecture, Planning Department, London, 1968-9.
Karla Kowalski runs a practice with Michael Szyszkowitz in Graz. The office was started in 1973 and now employs sixteen people. She is a Professor and Head of the Department of Public Buildings and Planning at Stuttgart University, West Germany. From 1969-71 she worked with Behnisch and Partners, Munich, on the Olympic Stadium, followed by one year lecturing at the Gesamthochschule in Kassel. She has lectured at departments of architecture in West Germany, Austria, Britain, Belgium, Norway and Switzerland
Selected work:
Mortuary Hall, Schwarzach/Pongau, 1977-8. Green house, Graz, 1978-9. Renovations and additions to Grosslobming Castle, 1979-81. Zusertal house, Graz, 1980-1. Renovations and additions to Pichl castle, Mitterdorf, 1982-4. 43 community dwellings at Alte Poststrasse, Graz, 1982-4 Red house, Graz, 1983-.4 House at Lustbuhel, near Graz, 1984-5. 24 community dwellings at Eisbach-Rhein, 1984-6. Insurance building reception area, Graz, 1985. Church and community centre, Graz-Ragnitz, 1984-7. Institute for Biochemistry, Graz, 1985-90. Exhibition design for *Witches and Magicians*, Styria, 1987. Harmisch house, Burgenland, 1987-8. Walch house, Wien Hietzing, 1988-9. Horst Ruckle team house, Wien Hietzing, 1988-9. 25 dwellings, Sandgasse, 1988-92. 60 dwellings at Knittelfeld,

Karla Kowalski and her husband, Michael Szyszkowitz, practice in Graz in the south east corner of Austria near the Yugoslav and Hungarian borders. Their work is always the product of joint thought and discussion and none of their buildings can be called 'hers' or 'his' - always 'theirs'.

Their approach to architecture is strongly emotional - a point which they cherish. Not only do they understand the need for architecture to draw a positive emotional response from the user, but try to harness their own emotional attitudes as a creative input to design.

They reflect, 'An architecture which is integral and complex has to be so in its aesthetics and form, in its planning and building process and in its intellect and emotion. Just as harmonic vibrations make a fundamental tone rich and full, so the lively atmosphere of a space and richness in design depends on the breadth of input.'

'We are now conscious of the original function of architecture, which consists not only in satisfying the basic needs of man, but also in stimulating him. Architecture *should* stimulate - and be a catalyst for mental, intellectual and emotional reactions and processes in us.'

'We want architecture to touch people again, and we try to create an atmosphere by architectonic means to produce psychological effects and provoke ideas. These things can only happen if we use the tricks of our job, and if they are good ones people can use architecture as a catalyst.'

There is a magical, and on occasion sinister, ring to the names of schemes undertaken by the practice; Grosslobming castle, Mortuary Hall in Schwarzach/Pongau, and the design of an exhibition in 1987 entitled 'Witches and Wizards' for the Styrian region of Austria. Nor does the magic end here, for their buildings explode from the ground bursting with energy and vitality. The strong use of the diagonal - whether for plunging rooflines, as at the preying mantis addition to Grosslobming Castle, or skyward shooting glazing on the Institute for Biochemistry - is a leitmotif on many schemes. This is dramatic architecture, intriguing and exciting, which demands a strong response from those who use it or pass by.

1988-92. German rheumatism research centre, Berlin, 1988-. International Garden Exhibition, 1989-93. Experimental housing, Stuttgart, 1989-.
Awards:
Eighteen First prizes in competitions, 1978-. including: Austrian prize for Mortuary Hall, Schwarzach, 1979. Geramb medal from the Styria region for a house above Graz, 1981. Geramb medal for Grosslobming Castle, 1982. Austrian Architects Association prize for Grosslobming Castle, 1982. Styrian region Great Award for Grosslobming Castle, 1983. Geramb medal for Pichl Castle, 1985. Special Award, the Greater Austrian housing prize, 1987. Austrian Architects Association prize for the Parish Centre, Graz-Ragnitz, 1988. Successful competition entries: The practice has been placed in fifteen competitions since 1975. These include ten first prizes, three second prizes and two third prizes. In 1987 the practice won three first prizes for housing in Knittelfeld, a regional hospital in Bruck and a secondary school in St Johann. In 1988 it came first for a rheumatism research centre in Berlin and second for housing in St Peter. There have been sixteen exhibitions of Szyszkowitz and Kowalski's work between 1983-8, in the United States, West Germany, Australia, France, Egypt, Scotland, Italy, Hungary, Belgium and Yugoslavia.

Grosslobming Castle

Institute for Biochemistry, Graz, 1985-90.

73

House, Wienhietzing,
1988-9.
Window detail

Church interior, Graz-
Ragnitz, 1984-7.

Harmisch house,
Burgenland, 1987-8.

Australia Eve Laron

Eve Laron

Biography
Born in Hungary in 1931.
In 1949 left Hungary on
foot with future husband,
walking through
Czechoslovakia to refugee
camps in Vienna. Lived in
Israel 1949-1955, and
arrived in Sydney, Australia
in 1955. Studied
architecture at night while
working during the day in
Haifa and obtained a B.A.
degree. Fellow of the Royal
Australian Institute of
Architects, F.R.A.I.A. and
an Associate of the Royal
Institute of British
Architects, A.R.I.B.A.
Worked on commercial
projects for several
architectural practices 1955-
1975. Made a Partner in
the firm Eric Towell and
Partners, Architects, 1973.
Studied Behavioural Science
at Maqarie University and
obtained a B.A. degree in
1979. Established own
practice as Eve Laron,
Architect, 1979. Awarded
the 'Excellence in Housing
Award', 1979. Founded
'Constructive Women', an
association of women
architects,planners and
women in the building
industry in 1983. Altered
the practice to Eve Laron
and Associates, Architects
in 1983. Included in
'Architect designed
Houses', 1989, an annual
publication of Architecture
Media Australia.
Recent work includes
housing designed
specifically to take account
of the landscape and

Eve Laron set up practice in 1979 on her own, specializing in housing design, after working for much of her career on commercial projects.

After training and working in a stimulating environment in Israel from 1949 - 1955 her arrival in Sydney proved a shock.

She writes of those early years, 'I was transported back into the Middle Ages. I was looked on as somewhat of a freak: a woman architect, married and with a small child to boot! In the Australia of the 1950s my place was firmly considered to be at home. But I was stubborn.'

In 1964 matters improved. Armed with photographs of her own newly constructed house, she landed a responsible job with a firm which valued her design abilities and there she progressed fast. Yet when in 1973 she was made a partner, two male associates of the firm resigned rather than work for a female boss.

'At first it was fun and tremendously satisfying,' she says, 'I could design unhindered and without interference. Eventually however the euphoria of "having made it" wore off and I began to be more and more dissatisfied with the totally and overwhelming masculine attitudes and atmosphere of the building industry in general and its effect on our cities in particular: the *man*-made environment was obviously and visibly unsatisfactory.'

Eve Laron's main concern is to develop an Australian architecture which transcends 'style' and responds to the way people feel about the environment in which they live. Her buildings allow for variations in climate by harnessing the power of sun, wind and water.

She comments that the crucial difference between Australia and other countries is that Australians have no suitable vernacular to fall back upon. Elsewhere, she maintains, traditional buildings have evolved naturally over the centuries and been shaped by the dictates of the climate - the well known and understood vagaries of wind, rain and sun. In addition, she argues, local masons and carpenters knew how to use and develop local materials and handed down the 'correct' way to build through many generations.

climatic conditions in which it is situated, and incorporates active and passive solar heating and water cooled rooms.

House 1, Sydney suburbs, New South Wales, Australia.

Left: House 2, Sydney suburbs.

Laron refers to the 'federation styles and outback homesteads, period pieces and old charmers,' as the vernacular styles of other countries imported by immigrants to Australia. She regards this as a tragedy as it stems from climates totally alien and inappropriate to the South Pacific.

The brick houses with narrow windows she so often sees remind her of inward looking buildings warding off North European weather - while all round her hibiscus blooms and bouganvillea runs riot.

She sees Australia as offering architects a unique challenge - the chance to develop an architecture pleasant to live in and fit for the climate, yet points out that so far they have failed their public as the vast majority of Australians make no use of them.

'Bauhaus', 'Federation', 'Post Modern', 'Cape Cod' or 'Modern Colonial' are the housing styles chosen by the Australian public for purely aesthetic reasons. As Laron argues, if architects have taught the public to appreciate buildings purely by their external appearance, rather than to understand that it is the user's comfort inside a building which matters, then it is not surprising that architects are so little used or appreciated, with honourable exceptions.

She refers to the fact that buildings can all too often cause people to feel claustrophobic, oppressed and alienated through inadequate consideration of scale, shape and materials. She insists that the scale should be human and the shape as intricate as possible.

In her own search for, and design of, humane architec-ture she considers the play of shade and sunlight, unexpected vistas, the sight of water, trees and sky. All these are considered important elements in creating an architecture which responds to people as they really are.

As a direct result of her own feeling of isolation Eve Laron initiated meetings of women architects which led to the formation of a discussion and support group. In 1983 'Constructive Women' (the Association of Women Architects, Planners and Women in the Building Industry) was born.

'At our first meeting 30 women turned up;' writes Laron, 'at our inaugural dinner six weeks later there were two hundred women architects, most of them in their late twenties or early thirties.'

'They looked at each other in astonishment and even though women constituted less than three per cent of the Australian architectural profession in 1989 it was still quite a number. They feel they have reached critical mass!'

Through group discussion they have understood that women bring a different approach to design - designing from the inside out, rather than from the outside in as they have observed their male colleagues do. Their plans are now to change the built environment for the better.

To quote Eve Laron, 'By reinforcing and supporting each other, by providing a forum for critical analysis, we should be able to humanize the city and restore the missing half of the equation, thereby improving the environment for men and women alike.'

77

Kenya

Diana Lee-Smith

Biography
Born in Britain in 1940.
Educated at the
Architectural Association
School of Architecture,
London, receiving the
A.A.Diploma in 1964.
Member of the Royal
Institute of British
Architects (R.I.B.A.), 1969
Member of the
Architectural Association of
Kenya (M.A.A.K.), 1986.
Awarded the R.I.B.A.
schools essay prize 1958.
Diana Lee-Smith is a self
employed architect in
Nairobi, Kenya. She is
principal of the firm Diana
Lee-Smith R.I.B.A.,
M.A.A.K.(A). She is a
member of the Board of
Directors of the Mazingira
Institute, Nairobi,1979-,
Editor of Settlements
Information Network Africa
(S.I.N.A.), 1981-, and co-
ordinator of H.I.C. (Habitat
International Coalition)
Women and Shelter
Network, 1988-. From
1964-9 she worked in
London for Chapman Taylor
Partners, Yorke Rosenberg
and Mardall and John
Winter Associates. From
1969-71 she was in charge
of the first year programme
at the Department of
Architecture, University of
Nairobi. In 1971 and 1972
she lectured at the
University of California in
Hayward and Berkeley,
U.S.A., and from 1972-5

'I see architecture as a specialized profession that provides good buildings as a service for the society that uses them,' writes Diana Lee-Smith. 'My training prepared me to think as a designer about the context of a building and to question the brief of a building. Subsequently I have become much more concerned about the social role of the designer and am trying to change the way in which our profession provides its services where they seem inappropriate to what the users need.'

'As early as 1969 I was aware that the broadest context we work in as professionals is the global environment and that we are responsible for designing in it and with it. People can be the most useful and adaptable part of the global environment.'

'In 1969 I took up the offer of a teaching job in the University of East Africa in Nairobi, Kenya. In post-independence Africa it was even more clear that the standard professional training would not do. The absolute poverty of the majority and the lack of developed building industries makes conventional solutions inaccessible, especially where they have a high foreign exchange cost. Anyway the spaces people want to live in are different depending on culture as well as economics. I try to provide useful professional services in a context where most people cannot afford either the buildings we design nor our fees.'

'I married a Kenyan and with other professionals we started a non-profit research and development organization. We try to provide information and a range of services that can improve the living situation of poor communities. For example, we are doing a rural housing improvement project in Western Kenya, on the border with Uganda, where we hope to improve local production of building materials and construction skills as well as housing, by working with local artisans and women's groups.'

'Since 1981 I have been the editor of Settlements Information Network Africa (S.I.N.A.), which links over 500 people and organizations in thirty two African countries doing this type of work, servicing self-help efforts of the rural and urban poor. We produce a newsletter, organize regional and national meetings and exchange visits and try to channel donor funds to grass roots organizations. Recently we have been promoting the growth and development of the housing and construction co-operative movement in Africa.'

'Since the United Nations International Year of Shelter for the Homeless in 1987, we have been in touch with similar organizations in other countries as active members of Habitat International Coalition (H.I.C.), the global non-governmental body concerned with the rights of the poor to a safe and secure place to live. Women predominate amongst the world's poor and homeless and we have linked

she taught in Toronto, Canada, at the University of Toronto and York University, Toronto. She was made an Assistant Professor at York University in 1973.
Selected work:
1964-69. Plastics Factory, Northumberland, 1965, Rochdale Further Education College, 1966, housing for the Harding Housing Association, London, 1967-9. 1977-89. Consultancy work for the Governments of Sweden, Zimbabwe and Kenya, supervision work for World Bank urban projects in Kenya, 1979-84, and a number of studies and projects for United Nations agencies, 1976-87. At the Mazingira Institute, Kenya, she has undertaken fourteen research and evaluation projects for organizations and universities throughout Africa looking into the questions of housing and supporting the poorest rural and urban members of society.
Awards:
Second place in the Athens Centre of Ekistics 'Le Corbusier' Prize, 1966. Commendation for the Berkeley Design Methods Group's Energy Conservation in Building Prize, 1975. Diana Lee-Smith has written for twenty nine books or journals around the world, 1984-9, and edited the first eighteen issues of S.I.N.A., Nairobi, 1982-9. She has also written twenty unpublished papers which were commissioned from her or are conference lecture papers, 1974-88.

up with others around the world to form the H.I.C. Women and Shelter Network. Our first newsletter was produced in English, French, Spanish and Portuguese in 1989.'

'All too often professionals form part of the bureaucratic block that prevents access for the poor to housing and other services because of outdated laws and procedures. During 1987 I was involved with the Architectural Association of Kenya and others in promoting a shift in thinking at the congress of the Union of International Architects (U.I.A.).'

'Once a year I do a comic strip which forms part of an information package that goes out to Kenyan and Uganda children. It covers health, nutrition and environmental issues. We collect information from the children, in the form of a competition, which increases our knowledge of local environmental and cultural traditions. The two characters in the strip, Mingu and Sweetie, are based on real children in our neighbourhood. Children like to read their adventures, and it is one of the few chances I get to do any drawing!'

Women upgrading their dwellings using traditional materials, Nairobi.

Demonstration house, Kariobargi Housing and Settlements Co-op. Beth Wambeii, chairwoman of the Co-op. The co-op has 526 members living in shanty dwellings. Members have manufactured materials used for the demonstration house.

USA   Diane Legge

Biography
Born in Englewood, New
Jersey. Educated at
Stanford University,
California, obtaining a B.A.
in architecture, 1972, and
Masters degree in
architecture at Princeton
University, New Jersey,
1975. Registered as an
architect in the States of
Delaware, Illinois,
Maryland, Massachusetts,
New Jersey, New York,
Ohio, Pennsylvania, Texas
and with the National
Council of Architectural
Registration Boards.
Member of the American
Institute of Architects
(A.I.A.)
Diane Legge joined
Skidmore Owings and
Merrill (SOM) in Chicago in
1977 and was made partner
in charge of design in 1982.
Much of SOM's work
covers a wide range of
commercial projects from
city centre hotels, offices
and apartment blocks to
airport facilities and
university campuses. The
practice's work spans the
world. In October 1989 she
left SOM to set up practice
on her own. She is on the
Board of Directors of the
Chicago chapter of the
A.I.A and on the Board of
Governors of the school of
the Art Institute of
Chicago. She is on a
number of committees
within the Art Institute of
Chicago dealing with film,
contemporary art, painting
and sculpture. She is a
visiting critic and lecturer at
schools of architecture and
on the advisory board of
Princeton's school of
architecture and urban
planning, and a thesis
advisor at the University of
Illinois, 1989-90.
Major projects on which
she has been involved
include: Bethesda Metro-
Development project; retail,
office and housing complex,
Bethesda, Maryland, 1989.
Herman Miller showroom
interiors, Chicago, Illinois,
1988. Master plan for
development of Arlington

Skidmore Owings and Merrill is renowned for its sophisticated office designs and large scale commercial developments which are to be found in city centres throughout the world.

Diane Legge was named partner in charge of design at S.O.M's Chicago office in 1982 and remained there until deciding, upon the birth of her second child, to set up her own practice in late 1989. The design partner at S.O.M. sets the standards of quality which must be met in each phase and detail of a project's execution, and leads the team, which may include many different disciplines and specialists, through a project from start to finish.

Since joining S.O.M. in 1977 Diane Legge has been involved in the development of large scale office, mixed use, residential and industrial facilities in the United States. Most of her work is in Chicago where she has contributed to Chicago's large body of modern buildings which are famed throughout the world.

She has assisted developers to present large scale urban projects, such as the extension of the McCormick exhibition centre and Riverfront office tower, to community groups in Chicago. She was asked to play a similar role in explaining the proposed retail, office and residential development to Bethesda residents for the Bethesda Metro Development corporation in Maryland.

Diane Legge's new printing plant for the Boston Globe newspaper in Billerica, 1984, won her an A.I.A. Distinguished Building Award. What might have been merely a vast shed for printing technology was transformed under her sure touch into a sophisticated and enjoyable place to work. Such was the client's reaction that she was asked to extend the newspaper's offices at a different site, and furthermore to act as design consultant for new printing facilities for the Philadelphia Newspapers Group.

The 1985 fire at Arlington International Racecourse provided Legge with the opportunity to design a new track and stadium. She shows a thorough knowledge of the excitement and procedures of a day at the races in her Arlington buildings. International flags flutter in the breeze, colourful striped awnings shade the spectators, while the stadium itself, unlike others built previously, allows racegoers a clear view of the paddock as well as of the track. They can therefore watch tension growing during the pre-race events of weighing in, saddling up and walking the horses on one side of the stadium before turning their attention to the other, and the race itself.

Park racetrack, Illinois, 1988. Renovation and addition to Coon Hall, Northwestern University, Evanston, Illinois, 1988. Office building for Manufacturers Hanover Plaza, Wilmington, Delaware, 1988. Master plans for Smith Kline and French laboratories in Philadelphia, Pennsylvania, Welwyn Garden City and Tonbridge Wells, England, 1987. Office buildings and interiors for Riverfront Park, O'Hare Plaza, Chemical Bank, Chicago, Illinois, 1986. Phase 2 office building for MidCon Corporation, Lombard, Illinois, 1986. McCormick Place Exhibition Centre extension, Chicago, Illinois, 1986. Master plan for a leisure and equine community and hotel, Lake County, Illinois, 1986. Feasibility Studies for office buildings in Chicago and Philadelphia, 1986. Olympia Centre retail, office and condominium complex, Chicago, Illinois, 1986. Executive office interiors for Mark Controls Corporation, Skokie, Illinois, 1985. Federal inspection facility at O'Hare International Airport, Chicago, 1985. Office and housing complex for Harvard University in Cambridge, Massachusetts, 1984. Hotel lobby and office renovation, Dallas, Texas, 1984. Boston Globe plant renovation and satellite printing facility Billerica, Massachusetts, 1984. Chicago Tribune printing plant, 1982, and Tribune tower renovation, Chicago, Illinois, 1984. Chicago central area plan, Illinois, 1983. Office buildings in New York, 1982.
Awards:
Masonry Institute Award, 1983 and 1984. Chicago Chapter of the A.I.A.: Young Architect Award, 1984. Distinguished Building Award, 1985, Interiors Award, 1989. Progressive Architecture First Award, 1984. Edison Award, Certificate of Merit, 1985. New York

Architectural League, 1986. American Institute of Steel Construction, Award of Excellence, 1987. ASHRAE Energy Awards Programme, Illinois Chapter, 1988. American Society of Landscape Architects Honor Award, Illinois Chapter, 1988. Friends of Downtown Honor Award, Honor Award, 1988. Diane Legge's work has featured in nine exhibitions between 1984 and 1989, and fifteen individual journals including *Progressive Architecture*, *Interiors* magazine and *Inland Architect*.

Above: Boston Globe Printing Plant, Billerica, Massachusetts, 1984. Exterior.
Right: Interior of the Boston Globe Printing Plant.

Left: Arlington International Racecourse, Illinois, 1988.

Spain   Sol Madridejos

Sol Madridejos

Biography
Born in Madrid in 1958.
Educated at the Escuela
Tecnica Superior de
Arquitectura (E.T.S.A.M.)
in Madrid qualifying in
1982.
Sol Madridejos is a principal
of Bau Arquitectos studio in
Madrid, which she, her
husband and colleagues
started in 1982. Founder
member of Studio
Européen d'Architecture
(S.E.A.), 1988.
Selected work:
Apartment conversion,
Madrid, 1983. ARCO '84
stand, Madrid, 1984. Court
building, Seville, 1984-6. 4
dwellings and a gymnasium,
Alicante, 1985-8. Martin's
apartment, Madrid, 1987.
Retirement home for the
elderly, Madrid, 1987-9.
Sanchi's apartment,
Madrid, 1988. Three
RESPOL-BUTANO office
renovations in Barcelona,
1988. Urban planning
schemes: Proposals for the
renovation of the Green
Belt in the South of Madrid
for the City Planning
Authorities. Planning
proposals for Veldemoro,
Madrid, 1986. Planning
proposals for the cities of
Banos de Rio, Tobia,
Boadilla, Albeida de Iregua,
Entrena and Tricio in La
Rioja region, 1986.
Awards:
Third prize in the
international competition for
the new Opera, Paris,
1983. The firm's work has
been exhibited in Paris in

Sol Madridejos started the Madrid practice, Bau Arquitectos, with colleagues in 1982.

Its name became known in 1983 when they came third in an international competition for the design of a new opera house in Paris. The French connection remains dear to Sol Madridejos' heart, and in 1988 she and her partners started a Franco-Spanish group.

'In the pursuit of my profession I attach the greatest importance to contact with other architects and artists', she writes, 'and to travelling to see buildings *in situ*. This is why after several trips, contacts and joint projects with young Parisian architects we formed the Studio Européen d'Architecture (S.E.A.)in 1988 for international activities connected with architecture. We are editing a publication and giving lectures in Madrid on ten young Parisian architects, with the aim of continuing the relationship between young French and Spanish architects which got underway with the Spanish Architecture Exhibition in Paris in 1984.'

Sol Madridejos likes to be in control. 'I have always taken a very demanding approach to a project, taking care of the entire process from conception to the construction of the last detail.'

'The most interesting projects I have worked on can be grouped under three headings:

1. The Court building in Seville, 1984-6, and the old people's home in Madrid, 1987-9, both of which I found particularly interesting as they share similar elements of space and construction.

2. A series of office renovations in Barcelona in 1988 for the Spanish multi-national company, RESPOL-BUTANO. These were small scale works which provided me with the opportunity to experiment with materials and detailing, which was helpful for later projects on a larger scale.

3. Urban planning. I am working on a large scale urban project in 1989 called the 'Green Belt' in the south of Madrid. The railway line, which until now has crossed this section of the city at ground level, is to go underground. This will lead to the recovery of a new city space in which a long belt will connect a variety of buildings, (offices, housing and so on), and new parks. It is the largest and most important urban project underway in Madrid, and the whole office is engaged on it.'

RESPOL – BUTANO office
reception area, Barcelona, 1988.

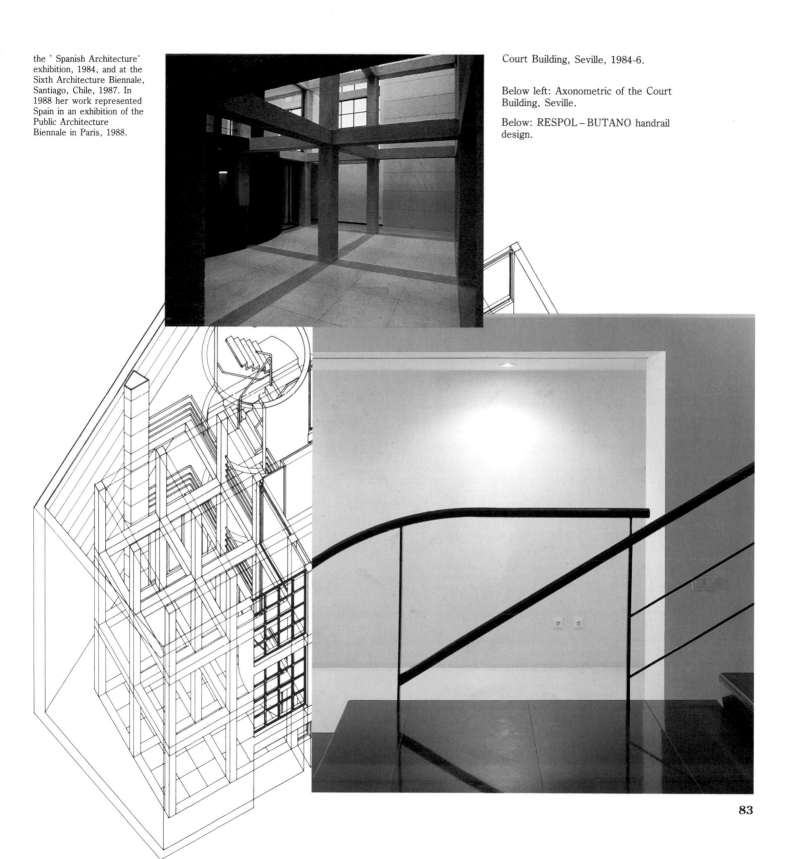

the ' Spanish Architecture' exhibition, 1984, and at the Sixth Architecture Biennale, Santiago, Chile, 1987. In 1988 her work represented Spain in an exhibition of the Public Architecture Biennale in Paris, 1988.

Court Building, Seville, 1984-6.

Below left: Axonometric of the Court Building, Seville.

Below: RESPOL – BUTANO handrail design.

83

Spain

Marta Maiz

Biography
Born in Tolosa in 1959.
Educated at the Polytechnic
University of Madrid (P.U.)
school of architecture
graduating in 1985. In 1984
she was awarded a grant
by the Spanish Government
Architects Department for
post-graduate studies.
Marta Maiz is a principal of
her practice which she runs
jointly with Enrique
Romero in Madrid. The
firm undertakes
architecture, urban
planning, industrial and
commercial work, interior
and graphic design. She
taught at the Polytechnic
University of Madrid school
of architecture, 1983-4, and
the school of design and
fashion, 1986-9. She has
lectured at the Paris-
Belleville school of
architecture, 1985.
Selected work:
3 family houses, Madrid,
1984-5. Guides for the
cities of Caceres, Granada,
Leon and Palma de
Mallorca for the Spanish
Ministry of Transport,
1984-5. House renovation,
Madrid, 1986. SOLANA
shops in Cordoba, 1985,
Barcelona, Bilbao, Oviedo,
1986, and Madrid, 1987.
BLANCO shops, Seville
and Valencia, 1986.
Renovation of the school of
Design and Fashion,
Madrid, 1986. Family
house, Pamplona, 1987.
Family house, Madrid,
1987. Gardens in Madrid,
1985 and 1989. Family
house, Burgos, 1988. Two
family houses, Madrid,
1988. Bus station, Madrid,
1987. Family house,
Burgos, 1989-90. VIKEX
factory, Madrid, 1989.
Family house, Avila, 1989.
Two family houses, Madrid,
1989. Proposals for 128
apartments,Madrid, 1989-.
Graphic design work for
SOLANA and BLANCO,
1986. Design for Castano
textile factory, Madrid,
1987. Telephone box
design, 1988-9.
Awards:
Commendation for the

There is one supremely important thing in Marta Maiz's life - and that is architecture.

'Whenever I am asked to talk about it I am unable to be anything but enthusiastic,' she declaims, 'I teach architecture, I create architecture and architecture envelops my daily life. The architect's craft is most gratifying: after a gestation period aspirations take form, they come to life and they EXIST.'

Marta Maiz, trained as an architect, and with a practice in Madrid which she and a partner jointly run, finds work in many fields of design. In the four short years she has been working she has carved a niche as an architect of twelve highly individual family houses, as an interior designer of seven fashion shops situated throughout Spain, as a designer of clocks, furniture and a telephone booth, and as a graphic designer of Spanish city guides and logos for assorted commercial enterprises.

She comments, 'In looking back over the varied nature and scale of the subjects I have had to deal with, I wonder about the role of the architect in today's world. Where does architecture begin, and where does it end? The individual is clothed in a succession of skins, from clothes to a house, from a house to the city, and intervention in any of these constitutes an architectonic act in the broadest sense of the term.'

Her family houses, factory and shop interiors show the flair and boldness which has come to be associated with modern Spanish design - strong geometric shapes, confident use of space, and dramatic dashes of colour. It is a style quite different from other Mediterranean countries, more reminiscent of that outpost of the old Spanish colonial empire known nowadays as California, than of close neighbours France or Italy.

design of the Spanish international exhibition pavilion, 1984. First prize for an exhibition stand for A.R.C.O.,1985. Marta Maiz's architectural work has been exhibited in Paris and Salamanca, 1985, and her design work in the 'Spanish Fashion' exhibition in Madrid, 1986. Her work has been published in seventeen journals, 1977-87, including *El Croquis* and *El Pais*.

Right: Cuadrado family house, Burgos, 1989. Left below: Cuadrado house interior, Burgos.

Right & below right:
VIKEX factory, Madrid,
1989.
Below: Telephone booth
design, 1988.

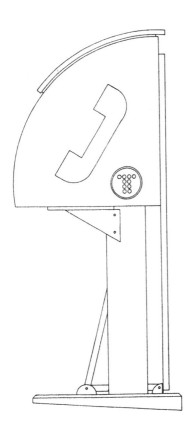

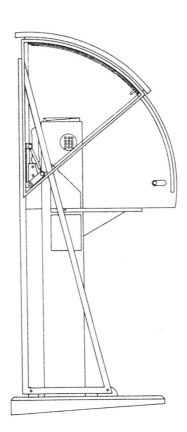

Below: Solana shop
interior, Barcelona,
1986.
Right: Solana shop
interior, Cordoba, 1985.

Sweden — Annalena Mosseen

Biography
Born in Gothland, Sweden, in 1952. Educated at the Royal Academy of Technology in Stockholm, obtaining a degree in architecture in 1976. Founding partner in 1980 of Visby Arkitektgrupp AB, Visby, Gothland. Visby Arkitektgrupp is the largest architectural office on the Baltic sea island of Gothland. It has nine partners, all on an equal pay and responsibility basis, and is made up of architects, engineers and interior designers. Prior to founding Visby, Annalena Mosseen worked for Coordinator Architects, Stockholm, and then for Ralph Erskine, Stockholm, on projects at the University of Stockholm. She turned down the offer of a partnership to return to Gothland.
Selected work:
New terraced housing for ABG municipal housing, Larbro, Gothland, 1981 and 1984. Mixed use commercial and residential renovation, Visby, 1982-3. Environmental improvements to the Grabo housing estate, Visby, Gothland for ABG housing association, 1982-6. Restoration of 'The Triangle', a central medieval area of Visby for the property owners, 1985-6. Factory extension and conversion into offices, Visby, 1987. Conversion of

Work for Ralph Erskine in Stockholm was coming to an end - it was time to return home.

In the summer of 1980 Annalena Mosseen returned to her birthplace, Gothland, an island jutting into the Baltic sea, to start an architectural practice with three other architects. Today Visby Arkitektgrupp is the largest practice in Visby, a city of 22,000 inhabitants. The nine partners, who work on an 'equal pay for all' basis include architects, engineers and interior designers. As the practice has grown so has its ability to tackle the complexities of working closely with housing tenants, in developing the precision needed for sensitive work in historical areas, and the patience to track down funding from various sources to make a previously untenable scheme feasible.

In 1982 Annalena Mosseen was contacted by ABG (Aktiebolaget Gotlandshem), the island's community housing association. It was concerned that it might find itself in a similar position to other housing associations in Sweden, with unpopular large estates containing difficult to let apartments. It wished to forestall what it saw as an almost inevitable period of decline. Mosseen and colleagues, in lengthy discussion with existing tenants at Grabo on Gothland, drew up a long list of proposals which challenged many management attitudes found within ABG. A four year plan was agreed and the 1800 tenants involved, who lived on two large estates, soon saw the promised improvements take place. 'Our tactics were simple ', reports Annalena Mosseen, 'we mobilized local radio, the press and schools for support and no sooner were the plans for a yard finalized (one estate alone had fourteen courtyards) than the work to be done was carried out. We held sixty meetings with tenants and not one courtyard turned out the same as another. Vandalism disappeared and people stopped moving away - both signs of increased harmony and comfort.'

A good number of the initial ideas which Mosseen had seen as improving the quality of life for tenants came to fruition; conference and hobby rooms, an outdoor swimming pool, a cafe and a sauna. Each building was designed with great care to provide a focus and enliven the somewhat bleak surroundings. Bay windows were added to the gable end of blocks to enlarge the apartments to a popular size and create lighter living rooms. Extra garages were provided, as was a caretaker's workshop, laundry rooms were redesigned to overcome problems and new uses were suggested for unoccupied apartments. Three of these were tested - a conversion of a ground floor apartment for a playgroup, the 'knock through' of two apartments to provide nursing care facilities for the handicapped, and an apart-

ment for termly rent by students and holiday let to tourists. A health centre is still to be built, but plans for a church did not survive.

The project aroused enormous interest. Other housing associations flocked to see how problem estates could be made successful, and the University of Lund, Sweden, is carrying out research into the project for the Swedish National Building Research Council.

Annalena Mosseen shows tenacity in all she tackles. Not content with proving that Grabo could become popular with its tenants, she turned her attention in the late 1980s to a run down medieval commercial and residential quarter of Visby known as 'The Triangle.' The area had become very dilapidated, suffering from frequent changes of ownership and subsequent lack of care. Loans for improvement were not readily available to the property owners, but Visbygrupp hunted them down through the Swedish government's support for preservation of areas of cultural and historical significance.

Once the finance had been secured, the architects tackled the conflicting requirements of historical accuracy, modern day use and official regulations. 'The Triangle' became a pilot project for historical renovation, and historical accuracy was the focal point in all discussion and agreement. The medieval pattern of shops and warehousing at lower levels with living quarters above was retained. Traditional materials and craftsmanship were used and the insertion of modern necessities, such as kitchens and bathrooms and high standards of heating, was undertaken with the utmost care. The learning process which the practice went through on this project, and the systematic documentation needed to ensure its successful completion, have been recorded by the Swedish council for building research.

In early 1990 the practice heard that it had won the prestigious Europa Nostra award for their work at 'The Triangle'.

a central city area into an entertainment centre, 1988. Staged conversion of a school near Visby, 1984-7. Construction of campsite facilities on Gothland. Extension for a computer company, Visby, 1987. Construction of a housing estate in Visby, 1987-9. Conversion of newspaper offices and historic buildings, Visby, 1987-8. Conversion of commercial and residential buildings, Visby,1989. Proposals for the improvement of Visby harbour, in conjunction with other practices on Gothland.

Awards:

1989 Europa Nostra award for 'The Triangle', Visby.

Left & right: New bay windows on the Grabo housing estate, Gothland.

The Triangle, Visby,
Gothland.

Before renovation.

90

Above: Courtyard at
Ringaren, Visby,
Gothland.

The Triangle, Visby, Gothland, 1985-6.
Rejuvenation of a triangular shaped group of medieval buildings.

Canada   Patricia Patkau

Biography
Born in Winnipeg, Manitoba in 1950. Educated at the University of Manitoba, Bachelor of Interior Design, 1973, and Yale University, Master of Architecture, 1978. She is a member of the Royal Architectural Institute of Canada and the Architectural Institute of British Columbia.
Ms Patkau has received six academic awards including the National Society of Interior Designers Award, 1972, the University of Manitoba Gold Medal, 1973, and the 'Central Mortgage and Housing Fellowship' two successive years running, 1977 and 1978. Patricia Patkau is a principal of Patkau Architects which has offices in Edmonton and Vancouver. The practice involves itself with all types of work, from housing and small scale offices to a school for the local Indian community in British Columbia. Before joining John Patkau in 1979, Patricia Patkau taught at Yale University from 1976-8 and then returned to Canada to work for Bell Spotowski Architects in Edmonton. Patricia Patkau continues her teaching. From 1984-7 she was a design critic at the University of British Columbia and at the University of Pennsylvania in 1987. At present she is an Assistant Professor at the University of California at Los Angeles (U.C.L.A.).She has lectured at Calgary, British Columbia, and Alberta Universities. In 1989 she was a juror for two architectural competitions.
Selected work:
Galleria condominium, Edmonton, Alberta, 1978. McGregor residence, Edmonton, Alberta, 1979. Riverdale Community Centre, Edmonton, Alberta, 1980. Driver examination offices in Fort McMurray and Grand Prairie, Alberta,

Patkau Architects was founded in Edmonton, Alberta in 1978 by Patricia and John Patkau. Edmonton is a northern and fairly isolated Canadian prairie city. Because of this isolation from architects in other cities the ideas and attitudes which are evident in the practice's work today have emerged slowly through a small ongoing body of work. They have been grounded, of necessity, primarily through the practical experience of building.

As Patricia Patkau has become more involved in teaching - she is currently in charge of first year students at the University of California at Los Angeles (U.C.L.A.) - she has found the need to define the practice's approach to design.

'We don't tend to work from an ideology or to believe in any single definition of what architecture is. Such positions seem to have the problem of narrowing the potential. Instead our emphasis is on those aspects which are particular to each project, be they local culture, history, site, climate, building context, programme, client, appropriate technology or whatever. Our attempt is to identify and extract what we call the ''found potential'' of each situation and give it expression through our designs.'

This ability to spot the possibilities and translate them, with a sure touch, into exciting and dramatic buildings can be clearly seen in the firm's work.

The Pyrch residence in Victoria, British Columbia, uses severe horizontal and vertical planes to contrast with, and draw attention to, the characteristics of the natural landscape - rugged massive rocks and sparse, thin Gary oaks.

The Kurstin house in Woodland Hills, California, is split by a ravine. The two sides of the house are connected by arching wooden bridges and the dramatic steepness of the site shows within the house. Gigantic shading devices screen the decks from the intense local heat, and incidentally are an amusing reminder of the owner's passion for fly fishing rods.

Patricia and John Patkau.

1981. Pyrch residence, Victoria, British Columbia, 1983. Apartment renovation, Toronto, Ontario, 1984. Porter/Vandenbosch residence, Toronto, Ontario, 1985. Appleton residence, Victoria, British Columbia, 1985. Green residence, West Vancouver, British Columbia, 1987. Ma residence,Vancouver, British Columbia, 1988. Seabird Island Indian School, Agassiz, British Columbia, 1989. Canadian Clay and Glass gallery, Waterloo, Ontario, 1989.
Awards:
Progressive Architecture citation for the Galleria condominium,Edmonton, Alberta, 1981. Canadian Architect Awards of excellence for Blue Quill school, Edmonton, Alberta, 1983; Pyrch residence, Victoria, British Columbia, 1984; Alberta Research Council research office,Edmonton, Alberta, 1984 and Kustin residence,Los Angeles, California, 1987. Canadian Wood Council First Award for the McGregor house,Edmonton, Alberta, 1984. First prize Canadian Clay and Glass Gallery competition, 1986. Governor General's Medal for Architecture for the Pyrch residence,1986. Architectural Institute of British Columbia Honour Award for the Pyrch residence, 1988. In a seven year period the firm's work has featured in seventeen publications and ten exhibitions including a national travelling exhibiton of the firm's work sponsored by the University of Toronto in 1988-9.

Above: Pyrch residence, Victoria, British Columbia, 1983. Front Elevation.

Right: Pyrch Residence, Victoria, British Columbia. Side elevation

Left below: Seabird Island Native Indian School, Agassiz, British Columbia, 1989- 90. Under construction. Model.

Kurstin Residence,
California, U.S.A.,
1989. Under
construction. Model
Kurstin Residence,
California. Section
showing the ravine
which divides the house
into two parts.

94

Seabird Island Native
Indian School, Agassiz,
British Colombia.
Balcony roof detail.

Seabird Island Indian school is a building for a native Indian group on the flat, exposed edge of agricultural land on Seabird Island in the Fraser River, British Columbia. Mainstream education as well as courses in native traditional crafts and language are taught at the school. The building is sited so that it hunches its back towards severe winter winds to the north and opens up to the classrooms on the protected southern side. The porch, running in front of each classroom, acts as a classroom extension and as the link with the salmon drying racks, the gardens and nature trails.

95

Elizabeth Plater-Zyberk

Biography
Born 1950 in Bryn Mawr, Pennsylvania. Educated at Princeton University, B.A. in Architecture and Urban Planning, 1972, and Yale University Master of Architecture in 1974. Elizabeth Plater-Zyberk is a member of the American Institute of Architects. Principal and Co-founder in 1980 of Andres Duany and Elizabeth Plater-Zyberk, Architects, with its main office in Miami, Florida, and two smaller offices in Boston and Maryland. The practice is well-known for its many town design projects such as Seaside, Florida, the internationally acclaimed development in which new compact communities are planned as an alternative to suburban sprawl. In addition to working on large scale urban schemes, it has also designed a number of award winning individual houses for clients in the Florida region. In 1976 Ms Plater-Zyberk was one of the founding partners of the firm Arquitectonica where she worked until setting up her current practice in 1980. In 1977 she founded the Architectural Club of Miami and remained its President from 1986 until 1988. In 1988 she was a resident at the American Academy in Rome. She currently sits on the board of Directors of the Miami Beach Design Preservation League and the Bakehouse Arts Complex and is a trustee of Princeton University until 1992. From 1984 onwards she has sat on many selection and advisory committees amongst which are the A.I.A. National Design Committee, 1985-6, the Louis Sullivan Award for Architecture, 1985, Coral Gables House Governing Board, 1986-7, and on the Design Advisory Committee for the Indiana State Office Complex, 1987-8. She currently is on the board of

Elizabeth Plater-Zyberk, once co-founder of Arquitectonica International with Laurinda Spear, is now Principal in her own firm and is a major contributor to the exciting architecture which has come from the Florida region of the United States during the eighties.

She and her partner, Andres Duany, through closely observing what people like and dislike in cities, and analyzing successful patterns of urban growth, have developed new ideas about urban form. They draw strength from noting the many slow layers of development in the traditional town, and use their extensive architectural and planning skills to respond creatively in their designs to the public's often observed distaste for many modern cities.

Their highly influential Florida new town design, called 'Seaside', has been widely praised by critics of architecture throughout the world, and far more importantly by its inhabitants.

The practice has designed and built a number of highly individual houses for clients, which like 'Seaside', have won many awards.

Both Plater-Zyberk and Duany are actively involved in discussion and development of the architectural profession, seeing this as an important part of their lives, and beside sharing the design and administrative responsibilities of the practice, the two principals maintain an active involvement in academia.

Plater-Zyberk is Associate Professor and Director of the Master of Architecture programme at the University of Miami. Duany travels to universities around the country; he has taught groups at the graduate schools of Harvard, Yale and Princeton amongst others. In addition they have produced a special graduate studies programme in suburb and town design for the University of Miami School of Architecture.

Plater-Zyberk states, 'The principals' teaching and practice are closely related, both part of a mission to produce alternatives to twentieth century suburban sprawl. The firm's work assumes that the documented ills of suburbia, such as social isolation, traffic congestion, the separation of the workforce from job locations, not to speak of visual blight, are potentially soluble in the design of focused and integrated communities using the traditional small town as a model. The method is being tested in town design projects ranging in size from sixty to three and a half thousand acres.'

Those currently under way include Belmont, Virginia; Riverfront, New Hampshire; Kentlands, Maryland; Mashpee, Massachusetts; Blount Springs and Tannin, Alabama; Friday Mountain, Texas, and others in which the firm's responsibilities include master plan design, zoning and architectural coding.

advisors for Tigertail Productions. During the nine year period 1980-89 she gave more than twenty five lectures at universities and institutions throughout the United States and in 1985 and 1989 was invited to speak at the Royal Institute of British Architects, London.
Awards:
Purchase award for an addition to the American Library in Berlin, 1989. Golden Aurora award from the South East Builders Conference for Seaside, 1988. National American Institute of Architects, award for Seaside, 1987. Governor's award, Florida State, for Seaside, 1986. *Builder* magazine Choice Design and Planning award, for Seaside, 1986. *Builder* magazine Builder's Best award. 1986. *Architectural Record Houses* award for Villanova House, 1986. *Architectural Record Houses* award for Hibiscus House, 1984. *Progressive Architecture* citation for Seaside town plan, 1983. *Architectural Record Houses* award for Hibiscus House, 1983. Rio Salado Chapter of the A.I.A. award for Urban Planning, 1987. Florida State A.I.A. award for Hibiscus House, 1985. South Florida Chapter of the A.I.A. awards for Westover House, Southern Star restaurant and 'The Decline of the Suburbs', 1986, and awards for Clary House, Villanova House, and Hibiscus House, 1985. Also awards for Galen medical building, 1984, Seaside town plan, 1983, and Charleston Place. The firm's work has featured in twenty one exhibitions during the last decade. In 1989 its winning entry for an addition to the American Library was shown in Berlin. Seaside featured in seven exhibitions within the United States during the 1984-7 period. In 1986 Elizabeth Plater-Zyberk was included in two '40 under 40' exhibitions; the work of architects under forty years old. The Cooper-Hewitt Museum, New York, and

Above: Socol House, Coral Gables.

FIRST FLOOR PLAN

KEY

1 LIVING ROOM
2 DINING ROOM
3 KITCHEN
4 BREAKFAST ROOM
5 FAMILY ROOM
6 GUEST ROOM

Far left: Hibiscus House, Coconut Grove, Miami, Florida.

Left: Socol House, Coral Gables, Florida. First floor plan showing the use of covered balconies to shade and encourage breezes around and through the building.

the Cuban Museum of Arts and Culture have also featured the work of the practice. Her work has been written about in over one hundred and thirty publications including books and magazines from countries around the world.

Seaside, Florida. Town centre.

Seaside, Florida. Walkway.

Villa Nova House, Key
Biscayne, Florida.

Clary House, Sanibel
Island, Florida.

Canada   Helga Plumb

Biography
Born in Austria, 1939.
Educated at the Technische
Hochschule, Graz, Austria,
1958-9, and the University of
Toronto, Bachelor of
Architecture, 1963, and
Master of Architecture in
Urban Design, 1967. Fellow
of the Royal Architectural
Institute of Canada.
Helga Plumb is principal of
the Toronto based firm
DuBois Plumb Partnership.
The practice covers a wide
range and scale of projects
including hospitals, university
buildings,housing and
institutional buildings. Ms
Plumb has lectured and
taught at a number of
prestigious architectural
schools in Canada and the
United States. She was an
Associate Professor at the
University of Waterloo,
Ontario, 1981-2, and a
Visiting Professor at the
Technical University of Nova
Scotia, Halifax, 1985-6. She
was an executive member of
the Toronto Society of
Architects, 1980, past
chairman of Humber College
Interior Design advisory
council, and is on the Board
of Directors of the Canadian
Wood Council and Sterling
Hall Boys School, Toronto.
Selected work:
Bloor Park Squash club,
Toronto, 1974. Cobblestone
tennis Club, Mississuaga,
1974. Government of Canada
Office building, North York,
1977. Grand River Cable TV,
Kitchener, 1978. Tom
Longboat Junior High
School,Scarborough, 1979.
Scaramouche restaurant,
Toronto, Ontario, 1980-1.
Metropolitan Toronto
ambulance service
headquarters, North York,
1981. St Andrew by the
Lake Anglican church,
Toronto Islands, 1981.
Oaklands condominium
apartments and terrace
housing, Toronto, 1981.
Camp Hill Medical Centre,
Halifax, Nova Scotia, 1983.
Darlington Generating
Station, Information centres
at Bowmanville, 1984 and
Newcastle, 1983. Tannery

Helga Plumb left Austria at the age of twenty and settled in Toronto in 1959, entering the second year of architectural training at the University of Toronto.

'I was the only woman training and architecture was not considered a woman's field. Some of my colleagues asked why I had not taken up teaching or nursing and there were general comments about the inappropriateness of women in architecture. However my limited understanding of English protected me somewhat and things have changed over the years.'

'During my final year I received wise advice from my thesis tutor, a young Australian, who convinced me that working out my own ideas was more important than shopping for approval amongst my teachers. I later discovered, when teaching at the University of Waterloo, that it is very difficult to discourage students from seeking approval from their tutors.'

'I then spent a period of practical work in Canada and the United States and in the mid seventies developed a long range development plan for a new large community college in Toronto. Teaching work grew and I joined the Toronto

practice of Fairfield DuBois, as it was then called. In 1980 I became a partner of the DuBois Plumb Partnership and have concentrated on building.'

The DuBois Plumb Partnership is one of Canada's most prestigious architectural firms. Like other practices building in a country with vast areas of free space, it has been able to build large scale new projects. Yet Helga Plumb is not entirely happy with the way architects have treated her home town.

'I am a strong believer that we should build upon and reinforce the past, rather than demolish the existing and start all over again. Unfortunately our economic system is not in sympathy with my concerns, and Toronto is in many areas torn apart by the many projects that focus in on themselves rather than relate to the city or neighbourhood as a totality.'

John Shepard office building, North York, Ontario, 1980.

Bay estates, Kingston, 1984.
All Saints Hospital,
Springhill, Nova Scotia, 1986.
Department of National
Defence training and
equipment buildings, 1986-9.
Souris Hospital, Price
Edward Island, 1988.
Reininger residence,
Newmarket, 1988. Bell
Canada offices and
telecommiunication centres,
1989. Canadian Embassy,
Beijing, China, 1989-.
Maternity Hospital, Halifax,
Nova Scotia, 1989-. Sayer
residence, Lake Simcoe,
1989-.
Awards:
O.M.R.C. Award of
Excellence for Joseph
Shepard Building, North
York 1978; Award of Merit
for Grand River Cable TV,
1979; Award of Merit for
Tom Longboat Junior Public
school, 1981. *Canadian
Architect* Design award for
the Oaklands Housing
project, Toronto, and the
Year Book award for
excellence, 1978. Silver
Hexagon international award
of excellence for The
Oaklands, Toronto, 1980.
Low Energy Building Design
award of excellence for
Joseph Shepard
Building,1980. Ontario
Association of Architects
Design Award for the
Oaklands Housing Project,
1983. Governor General's
Medal for Architecture for
the Oaklands Housing
project, 1983. Toronto
Historical Board Award of
Merit for St. Andrew by the
Lake church, Toronto, 1985.
Nova Scotia Association of
Architects Award of Merit
for the Souris Hospital,
1988. A.I.A. Honourable
mention for health facilities
design at Souris Hospital,
1989. Helga Plumb's work
has featured in international
architectural publications and
been the subject of
television programmes. Her
work features in three
books, *Energy efficient
Buildings*, McGraw Hill,
1980, *Modern Canadian
Architecture*, Hurtig
Publishers, and *Low energy
Building Design Awards*,
published by the Canadian
Ministry of Public Works.

Oaklands Condominiums, Toronto, 1981.

Interior of Oaklands Condominiums, Toronto.

India   ## Madhu Sarin

Madhu Sarin

Biography
Born in India, 1945.
Educated at the Punjab
University, Chandigarh,
Bachelor of Architecture,
1962-7. Post graduate
diploma in Tropical Studies,
Architectural Association
School of Architecture,
London, 1969-70. Awarded
the gold medal for
outstanding student, 1967, at
Punjab University,
Chandigarh. Award from the
Environment Society of
Chandigarh for
environmentally related work
in Sukhomajri and Nada
villages, 1983. Vishwakarma
Award for professional
excellence, 1989.
Madhu Sarin is an architect
in private practice,
Chandigarh. She returned to
Chandigarh in 1977 after
seven years working in
London, 1970-77, as a
consultant to the United
Nations Economic and Social
Commission for Asia and the
Pacific (U.N.E.S.C.A.P.)
responsible for co-ordinating
a study on policies towards
urban slums and squatter
settlements. She has
continued to work as an
advisor to the Indian
Government and international
organizations as well as
directly with poor
communities in the Punjab
and Rajasthan.
    In the early eighties she
designed a fuel efficient
cooking stove, the Nada
Chulha, which has been
widely adopted in developing
countries. In the late
eighties she helped the
same communities with the
design and construction of
housing, environmental
rehabilitation and organizing
women as creative members
of the labour force. She
worked for MacManus and
Partners, London, from 1970-
3, and the Development
Planning Unit of London
University, 1973-7. During
this period she lectured at
the architecture departments
of the Oxford Polytechnic,
the South Bank and North
East London Polytechnics,
Bouwcentrum International
Education, Rotterdam,
London School of Economics
and the University of
Birmingham. From 1978-80
she worked with a team on
housing proposals for Bihar

In 1989 Madhu Sarin was awarded the Vishwakarma Award for Professional Excellence by the University of Chandigarh. It was named after Vishwakarma, the celestial architect of Hindu mythology, and the citation states that 'architecture is an all encompassing creative discipline spanning all the major fields of human endeavour - science, art, humanities and technology. With its perennial inspiration from a cosmic order, architecture becomes a 'habit of the mind' - propelled by an inner satisfaction.'

This interpretation of architecture accords with Madhu Sarin's views. She has always been concerned to use her architectural training in ways which effectively serve those who most need her professional skills - the poorest members of developing countries.

She writes, 'I feel that too often we get trapped in artificially designed disciplinary boundaries which neither permit us to understand problems in their totality nor explore our creative potential. I am happy to have transcended those boundaries and now feel no inhibitions in taking up issues which would normally not be linked to architectural practice by any stretch of the imagination. But, to me, architecture is an all encompassing discipline concerned with a search for the meaning in life.'

She has taken her deepening understanding of the structures which trap the poor in an apparently unending cycle of poverty and deprivation and devised solutions which involve the participation, commitment and training of local people - and they work.

Her response to the fuel crisis in the Shiwalik foothills of the Himalayas - the design of a fuel efficient stove known as the Nada Chula - has improved the lives of thousands of people living in many parts of the world where deforestation has occurred.

'Starting to work with rural women from 1980 has provided me greater space in working with people at grassroots, understanding their problems and using my professional skills to help develop strategies aimed at confronting some of these problems. Developing an improved cooking stove in collaboration with village women, and later designing a dissemination system for the stove through a decentralized network of trained women stove builders, was a rich and satisfying experience. Through it one gained much deeper insights into women's lives and a major part of my present work, together with my colleagues, is to work towards organizing the women to start dealing with their innumerable problems.'

'Simultaneously, working in backward rural areas with essentially subsistence economies has got us deeply involved with environmental issues and developing strategies for improved natural resource management. For people subsisting on their natural resource base, health of the environment concerns not just the quality of life but sheer survival. It is because of the destruction of natural forests in South Rajastan that we are forced to search for alternatives to the traditional timber and tile roofing system. Although not entirely satisfactory yet, our ferrocement roofing components are generating a lot of interest among local people and the local mason we have trained is likely to emerge as a creative and practical 'people's architect' in the area.'

The improved 'Nada Chula' cooking stove in a kitchen designed by the woman herself.

state, India. She was also a fellow of Urban Development at the Punjab State Institute, advisor to the Mexican Government and visiting lecturer in Britain and Holland. From 1980-3 she worked for the Ford Foundation in Chandigarh with responsibility for working with women at field level in the Himalayan foothills. This included the construction of earth dams to store and retain water,improving the agricultural economy, social forestry, employment generation and development of the Nada Chulha stove.

Sarin developed and promoted the stove in India and internationally. She has spoken at conferences in Sweden, Japan, Thailand, Holland, Britain, Pakistan, Hong Kong, Guatemala and Argentina about its application in developing countries. Member of a panel on rural energy set up by the Indian Government, 1983-. In 1987 she was called to a meeting with the Prime Minister of India to discuss the needs of the poor and in 1988 was appointed a member of the Indian Ministry of Education's National Resource Group to work on a project called 'Education for Women's Equality.' In 1988 she was appointed a member of the 'All India Council for Technical Education'.

Selected work:
1968-73. Building in Italy, and London. 1978-. Design and practical advice on housing with self help communities. Responsible for finding alternatives to traditional use of timber in construction in areas denuded of all vegetation. Development of cast ferrocement roofing system. Madhu Sarin has written for thirty publications, 1977-88. Five publications are about Chandigarh, capital city of the Punjab, and twelve concern the Nada Chulha stove.

Above: Ferrocement roofing shells cast using earth moulds.   Below: Self-Build settlements. Roof shells being installed.

103

Switzerland **Beate Schnitter**

Biography
Born in Switzerland in 1929.
Educated at the
Eidgenossische Technische
Hochschule Zurich
(E.T.H.Z), Diploma of
Architecture, 1954. Member
of the B.S.A. and the S.I.A.
Beate Schnitter started her
own practice in Zurich in
1955. She employs from 2
to 6 people. Teaches art
history and building
preservation at the
Interkantonales Technikum
Rapperswil. She lectures
frequently and is an advisor
to Schweizer Heimatschutz,
1973-. She is a member of
Inventar der
Schutzwurdigen Ortsbilder

Beate Schnitter's aunt, Lux Guyer, was Switzerland's first woman architect. She influenced Schnitter's life profoundly by offering a role model for her and insisting that she start her own practice, which Schnitter did in 1955 after completing her training.

As a child Schnitter lived in Holland, Ireland and France before and during the second world war as the family followed her father's work.

'I regularly visited my father's building sites, be it the Dunkirk West Pier or the Rotterdam car tunnel and I saw my aunt's new houses when on holiday in Switzerland. It was clear to me at a very early age that architecture was going to be my profession.'

'After Lux Guyer's death I followed her explicit wish and started my own office designing houses and apartments for friends. Competition wins helped bring in further work and although I have always felt the support of my colleagues this is not the case with politicians and businessmen in my country. ''You are the last person I would have thought of entrusting this project to'' came as a response to one commission I received. I find this attitude still prevalent when consulting county council and planning officers, after all most top positions in Switzerland are still firmly held by men.'

'My medium is space. Not simply an object's three dimensional form (as seen from the outside like a sculptor's work), nor just the space between objects nor the internal play of light, but all these elements working together as can be experienced by moving around inside the work. I like spaces which can work in a number of different ways. For example if a room has two doors it can be entered from either and seen as quite a different space. In designing room shapes I try to allow occupants the freedom to find their own uses and deployment of space.'

'I try to keep the personalities of old houses while adapting them to today's demands. In my early years I built apartments, housing estates and holiday homes and collaborated on the plans for a new suburb of Zurich to house ten thousand people. Now restorations and conversions of large, old houses take up most of my time.'

'As a board member of a housing co-operative I help my colleagues develop low rise, high density schemes and assess whether or not a village will go on the national register of historic places for Schweizer Heimatschutz, which is an organisation rather like the British Civic Trust. I do research and publish articles on the relationship between old and new development. We cannot continue to build on agricultural land, rather we should revitalise areas of villages and towns while taking care of their historic features.'

'This, to my mind, is the most important field for future architects.'

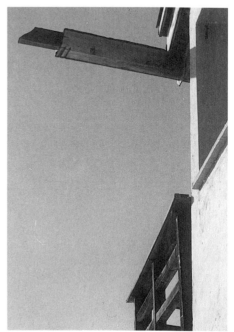

Above: House renovation near Zurich, 1986.

House in the Grisons, 1962-3.

der Schweiz (I.S.O.S) and advises townships on development in historic town centres; Kusnacht, Uitikon, Oberglatt, Weiningen, Waedenswil, Zurich and Neuenhof.
Selected work:
20 houses and holiday homes in Switzerland, Canada and France, 1955-75. Apartments and housing estates in Egg, 1963, Kusnacht, 1969-50, Stafa, 1973-8, Adliswil, 1963-74. Adaption and restoration of old buildings in Rapperswil, 1968-9, Schwyz, 1972-3, Kusnacht, 1973-6, Affoltern am Albis, 1973-77, Trinmulin, 1974-5, churches in Andermatt, 1977-82, Altendorf, 1977-8, Vorderer Florhof Zurich, 1979-83, Arosio, 1979-82, Rheineck, 1980-3, Boldernhaus Zurich, 1984-5, and Meilen, 1986-8. A vast number of conversions and renovations.
Awards:
Competition successes in Adliswil, Stafa, Leimbach, Wettswil, Affoltern am Albis and Zurich. She has written for *Heimatschutz* and Swiss newspapers and published a lecture on opportunities for women architects in *Frauen-Realität-Utopie*. Her work was exhibited in 1959 in Zurich and at the Basle Architecture Museum in 1989 at the time of the Ladies First architectural forum in Zurich.

Left: House in Toruls, Grisons, 1968.
Right: Detail of house in the Grisons.

Siegel Diamond Architects

Biography
Margot Siegel
Educated at the Pratt Institute, Bachelor of Architecture, 1955. Registered as an architect in California, New York, and with the National Council of Architects Registration Boards. Member of the A.I.A. Founding member of Siegel Diamond Architects in 1985.
Prior to this she ran her own office for fourteen years in Los Angeles concentrating on public service buildings among which were child care centres for the YMCA in Centinela Valley, California, and a community recreation complex at Lawndale, California. She also worked for a number of large Los Angeles based architectural practices on construction documents and administration for large scale commercial work which included a fashion mall in Queens, New York; commercial building complex in San Jose, California, and multi use complex in central Salt Lake City, Utah. Siegel was founder of the Los Angeles community design centre and is a commissioner on the Los Angeles county citizens planning council.She is a transportation commissioner for the city of West Hollywood. She has lectured at several Californian universities.
Katherine Diamond
Educated at the Technicon, Israel Institute of Technology, Bachelor of Architecture, 1978. Registered as an architect in California and Israel. Member of the American Institute of Architects. Founding member of Siegel Diamond Architects in 1985. Before joining Margot Siegel, Katherine Diamond worked in Israel from 1973-9 followed by a six year period with Benton/Park/Candreva in Los Angeles, California. During this time she was

Siegel Diamond Architects is an one hundred per cent woman owned architectural firm in Los Angeles, California.

The practice has chosen to concentrate on community care buildings for the University of California and elementary and junior high schools in Los Angeles, but as work floods in so the partners are widening their scope to encompass commercial, transportation and industrial projects in the Los Angeles region.

The two partners, Margot Siegel and Katherine Diamond, divide the practice's responsibilities; Margot Siegel is partner in charge of quality review and Katherine Diamond is partner in charge of design. They both bring different skills to the twenty person firm, which was started in 1985 with a third partner, Norma Sklarek, who left the practice in 1988 to pursue the end of her working career on the large projects - fifty million dollars upwards - which she most enjoyed.

Margot Siegel brought thirty one years work experience with her to the new firm. Prior to forming Siegel Diamond Architects she often worked on commercial and financial developments and through this developed skill and interest in translating designs, on occasion by other architects such as Frank Gehry and Cesar Pelli, into buildable schemes. This stage of a design - the translating from dreams to reality through the production of working drawings - is always complicated and burdensome. Margot Siegel continues this often unappreciated and unsung role for Siegel Diamond.

Katherine Diamond, partner in charge of design, takes the client's ideas and shakes them into shape.

Her architectural career started in Israel where, upon qualifying, she joined the armed forces and designed housing for the army and airforce. On her return to America she worked in Los Angeles on award winning high tech office complexes before becoming one of the founding partners of Siegel Diamond Architects.

The firm is growing fast and exudes an air of vitality which is both heard in conversation and seen in its buildings. The average size of projects grew between 1985 and 1989 from one million to four million dollars with the largest being more than double that size.

In 1989 the firm had the following projects in the pipeline: a new civic centre for the City of Lawndale, California, involving the renovation of, and additions to, the city hall, health centre and library. It also included proposals for a new civic square. There were two primary schools, Jefferson Elementary in Los Angeles and a multi purpose addition to the Commonwealth Elementary school in Los Angeles, while at Irvine, the University of California commissioned the practice to design a counselling centre and a child care centre for 120 young children.

In complete contrast, the partners turned their hand to designing four stations for the Long Beach - Los Angeles light railway. But, as with many American city attempts to provide successful public transport, the spirit is willing but its future unclear.

project architect for three award winning schemes, the Park beyond the Park complex, a Personnel support facility in Fort MacArthur, and the Otto Nemenz International building. She was president of the Association of Women in Architecture from 1985-7 and is on the advisory committee for Woodbury University's school of architecture. She is an active member of the A. I. A. serving as chairwoman of the Los Angeles chapter.

Selected work:

Jefferson new elementary school Number 1, Los Angeles, California. Child care centre for the University of California at Irvine, California. Lawndale civic centre project, Lawndale, California. Commonwealth elementary school multi purpose building, Los Angeles, California. Addition for Le Conte Junior high school, Los Angeles, California. Counselling and resource centre at the University of California, Irvine, California. Parking for U. C. L. A. , Los Angeles, California. Four light railway stations on the Long Beach - Los Angeles railway, Los Angeles, California. Municipal access studio for Los Angeles city department of communication, California. Osage Place low cost housing for the Community Development Commission of the County of Los Angeles, California. Bel Villagio condominium, Los Angeles, California. Mar Vista Lofts townhouses, Mar Vista, California. Sugar Hill Development, old people's housing and retail development Los Angeles, California. Richstone family centre for abused children and their families, Los Angeles, California. H. H. Lasher Road fifty unit old people's housing project, Los Angeles California. H. H. Lasher Road office complex, Los Angeles, California.

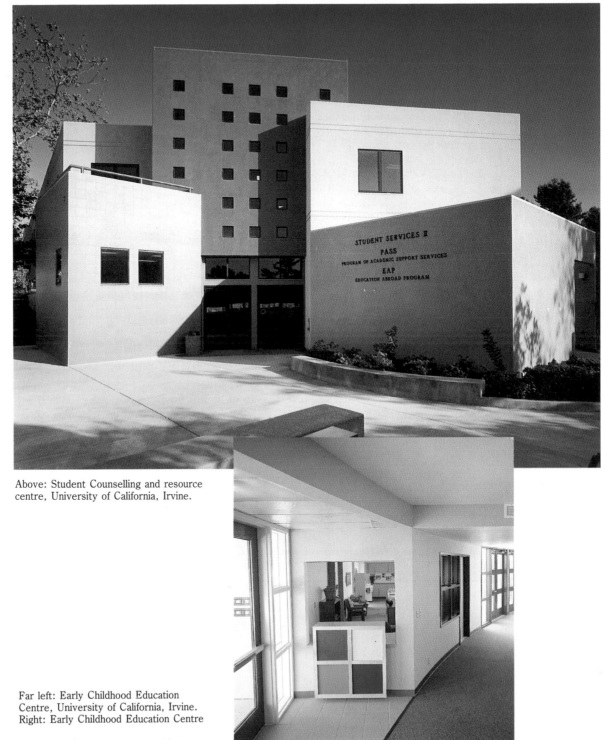

Above: Student Counselling and resource centre, University of California, Irvine.

Far left: Early Childhood Education Centre, University of California, Irvine.
Right: Early Childhood Education Centre

107

USA   Laurinda Spear

Biography
Born 1951 in Rochester,
Minnesota, USA. Educated
at Brown University,
Providence, Rhode Island,
BFA and Columbia
University, New York,
Master of Architecture.
Member of American
Institute of Architects,
Registered Architect in
Florida and New York;
National Council of
Architectural Registration
Boards Certification.

Since the inception in 1977 of Arquitectonica International, Laurinda Spear, one of the founding Principals, has been at the forefront of the firm's growth and its expansion from an initial base in Miami to the opening of three more offices in New York, Chicago and San Franciso.

The unconstrained and dramatic images Arquitectonica offers to its clients is immediately challenging and attracts the attention of the public, corporations and the media. Not all are pleased by what they see, but with a string of architectural awards behind it the firm has grown from strength to strength, tackling projects of increasing size and complexity.

Arquitectonica uses latest technological developments to their fullest extent and its buildings show a brash individuality and confidence which belie the degree of thought put into the firm's design processes.

As Laurinda Spear reflects, 'Arquitectonica's work is contextual. It recognizes place and time as two equally important elements of context. Its architecture seeks to capture the intangible spirit of place and time. In the search for that spirit, Arquitectonica analyses climate, topography and vegetation as well as culture, history and attitudes. The end result is new architecture that the community can embrace as its own, and whose permanence is attained by sensitively defining its place in history.'

The three buildings illustrated show tremendous verve and certainty in designing dramatic form. The Banco de Credito slices through Lima's city centre and incorporates an elliptical glazed light shaft into which a death defying balcony is slotted from which the observer can watch people ascending on an escalator far below.

The Centre for Innovative Technology in Virginia appears to defy all the laws of gravity as it leans dangerously outwards - an inverted truncated cone standing as proof of structural expertise. Meanwhile the North Dade Justice centre, bearing security in mind, presents few windows to the outer world.

Banco de Credito, Lima, Peru, 1988. Interior. A 530,000 square foot, four storey building designed as a headquarters for Peru's largest private bank and including a computer centre, two restaurants, auditorium and roof top health centre.

Principal and co-founder in 1977 of Arquitectonica International Corporation, with offices in Coral Gables, Florida, New York, Chicago and San Francisco employing over eighty architects, planners, designers and related professionals. Arquitectonica's work spans across the United States and several foreign countries. Its projects are diverse, ranging in scale and content from private homes and high rise apartment buildings to office towers, hotels, shopping centres and institutional buildings. Other design work includes ties, furniture, china and jewelry. Ms Spear has taught at the University of Miami and lectured internationally on Arquitectonica's work.

Awards:
Rome Prize in Architecture, 1978: *Progressive Architecture* design award citations in 1978 and 1980. *Architectural Record* award for Casa Los Indes, 1986. *American Institute of Architects Awards*: Florida Chapter Honor award for Overseas Tower office building, Dade County, 1982. South Florida Chapter for The Palace apartment block, Miami, Overseas Tower and The Square shopping centre at Key Biscayne, 1982, and The Atlantis apartment building, 1983. Virginia Chapter Honor award for the Centre for Innovative Technology, 1989. Florida Chapter Honor award for North Dade Justice Centre, 1989. Florida Chapter Honor award for Rio shopping complex, Atlanta, Georgia, 1989. Florida Chapter Honor award for the Miracle Centre mixed use complex, Miami, 1989. Florida Chapter Honor award for the Banco de Credito corporate headquarters, Lima, Peru, 1989.

Exhibitions:
New Americans, Rome, Italy, 1979. Cooper-Hewitt Museum, New York, 1979. AIA, Florida Chapter, Orlando, 1979. Pennsylvania

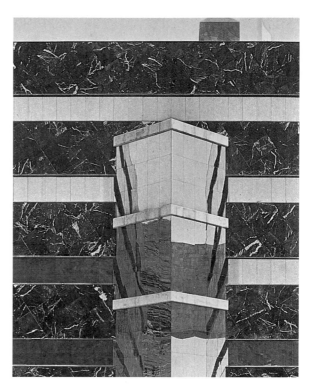

Above: Banco de Credito. Interior light well.
Above right: Banco de Credito. Exterior window detail.

Right: Center for Innovative Technology, Fairfax and Loudon Counties, Virginia.

State University, 1980.
Young Architects, Yale
University, 1980. University
of Virginia, 1981. Princeton
University, 1981. Columbia
University, 1982. Biennale
de Paris, 1982.
Contemporary Arts
Museum, Houston, Texas,
1982 Mandeville Art
Gallery, San Diego,
California, 1983. Hudson
River Museum, 1983. Ewald
Scholars symposium, Sweet
Briar College, 1983. Centre
for the Fine Arts, Miami,
Florida, 1984. Fort Wayne
Museum of Art, Fort
Wayne, Indiana, 1985.
Walker Art Centre,
Minneapolis, Minnesota,
1985. Sarah Campbell
Blaffer Gallery, Houston,
Texas, 1985. Institute of
Contemporary Art,
Philadelphia, Penn, 1986.
Arquitectonica, Buenos
Aires, 1987. Bass Museum,
Miami Beach, Florida, 1988.

Above & below: North
Dade Justice Centre,
Miami, Florida, 1988.
This regional courthouse
serves as an anchor for
a new government
centre complex. The
courtroom wing hovers
above two separate
buildings containing
court offices and a
secure receiving area.
'Arquitectonica's
architecture seeks to
capture the intangible
spirit of place and time.
In the search for that
spirit Arquitectonica
analyses climate,
topography and
vegetation as well as
culture, history and
attitudes. The end
result is new
architecture that the
community can embrace
as its own, and whose
permanence is attained
by sensitively defining
its place in history.'

Arc en Rêve, Bordeaux, France, 1988. Galerie Westersingel 8, Rotterdam, Netherlands, 1988. Gemeente Bibliotheek, Middleburg, Netherlands, 1988. Ontvangsthal Veldkamp, Raalte, Netherlands, 1988. Institut Français d'Architecture, Paris, France, 1988. Arkitekturforum, Zurich, Switzerland, 2989. Stadt Frankfurt am Main, Frankfurt, West Germany, 1989.

Centre for Innovative Technology, Fairfax and Loudon Counties, Virginia. The joint headquarters for the Commonwealth of Virginia's Centre for Innovative Technology and Software Productivity Consortium.The group of buildings includes an exhibition hall, classrooms, auditorium, press and briefing rooms.

Banco de Credito, Lima, Peru, 1988.

Britain

Susan Stewart

Biography
Born in Britain in 1953. Educated at Birmingham Polytechnic obtaining the Ordinary and Higher National Certificate (O. N. C. and H. N. C.), 1972-4, and the Oxford School of Architecture, 1980-2. Diploma in Architecture, 1982. Member of the Royal Institute of British Architects (R. I. B. A.). Chairman of Buckinghamshire Society of Architects, 1989. Susan Stewart is a Senior Architect with Buckinghamshire County Council responsible for the design of schools and libraries.
Selected work:
Priory Common First School, Milton Keynes, 1985. Ashbrook First School, Milton Keynes, 1986. Aylesbury Lending Library, Aylesbury, 1987. Aylesbury College major extensions, Aylesbury, 1987. Holmwood First School, Milton Keynes, 1988. Shenley Lodge Combined School, Milton Keynes, 1989-. Iver Heath Library, Iver Heath, 1989-.
Awards:
Second place in Glasgow School of Art Campus competition, 1986. Selected for the R. I. B. A. 'Forty under Forty' exhibition, 1988. She was subject of an article on women architects in the *Times*, 1988.

Working in the public sector as an architect for the local council is something of a rarity in Britain nowadays. As capital expenditure budgets have been slashed, so too have the architects departments of many boroughs and county councils throughout the length and breadth of the country.

There are however pockets of resistance, and happily Buckinghamshire, a relatively affluent area to the west of London, still has its own team of architects. Susan Stewart is pleased to work in the public sector, for Buckinghamshire County Council, while recognizing the reality of being part of a large, cumbersome bureaucracy.

'Working in the public sector is a continual conflict between opportunities and frustrations: the opportunities to do "good" work, both architecturally and socially, and the frustrations of being part of a large organization dealing, in the best way we can, with an enormous range of problems.'

'I have had opportunities to design major new-build projects since shortly after joining Buckinghamshire County Council, without having to spend time hunting for them. On the downside, the formalization of client relationships in which the building user is several times removed from the direct client with whom I am in contact, is a distinct problem. On schools, which are designed to provide a background for a child's development, the client is an educational advisor and the head teacher is not appointed until almost all major design decisions have been taken. Then the newly appointed head, keen to influence events, often expresses strongly conflicting views to the educational advisor on those few decisions that remain, despite or indeed because of his or her exclusion from all the early parts of the design process.'

'My most successful buildings have, I am convinced, often resulted from occasions where this process has somehow been circumvented. The long process from early discussions to feedback on use is a difficult one for all architects, and the build up of trust with one or two people who also see the project all the way through makes a great difference.'

'This process, from inception to realization, sets architecture apart from most other arts and can be draining. It is essential to keep personal control of all aspects of the process (from building details to the management of project costs) if one's design is not to be compromised by others. Indeed I take almost as much satisfaction from never having overspent a budget as I do from the quality of the completed product - well almost !'

Aylesbury College, Aylesbury, Buckinghamshire, 1987.

Major extensions.
Holmwood First School,
Milton Keynes.
Exterior.

Priory Common First
School, Bradwell, Milton
Keynes, 1985.
Courtyard.

USA Jane Thompson

Biography
Educated at Vassar College,
B. A. completed in 1947.
Masters Courses at New
York Institute of Fine Arts,
1951, and at Bennington
College, Vermont, 1961.
Jane McC. Thompson is
Vice President and partner
in Benjamin Thompson
Associates Inc. ,
Cambridge, Mass. She has
worked with Benjamin
Thompson Associates since
1969 and been Vice
President since 1978. Her
work with the firm involves
developing concepts for
mixed use urban planning
schemes in city centres
across the United States.
Her particular emphasis and
specialization is in
merchandising and retail
planning. She has been
closely involved in the
development of the
following urban planning
schemes: Revitalization
concept, merchandising and
public space planning at
Faneuil Hall Market Place,
Boston, Massachusetts,
1966- 78. Thematic design
concepts, Islamic decorative
Arts Programme,
InterContinental Hotels,
Abu Dhabi and Al Ain, U.
A. E. 1974-82. Urban site
planning, Ordway Music
theatre, St Paul, Minnesota,
1979-85. Concept and retail
planning at the Pavilion at
the Old Post Office,
Washington, DC, 1981-4.
Merchandise planning at
Ghiradelli Square, San
Francisco, California. 1983-7.
Revitalization concept at
Union Station, Washington,
D. C. , 1984-8. Community
and town centre planning at
the Royal Victoria Docks,
London, 1984-88.
Merchandising and tenant
selection at Century City
Marketplace, Los Angeles,
California, 1985-7. A master
plan for the streetscape and
urban environment in Grand
Central Business District,
New York, 1986-92 (Project
director). Community, retail
and public space planning at
the Customs House Docks
Development, Dublin, Eire,

'What women in architecture can and *must* contribute to our built environment has been a key issue in my career as both an architectural writer and a practitioner, as well as a determinant of my highly personal approach to design,' writes Jane Thompson. 'This starts with the belief (a minority view, I suspect) that architecture is not valid purely as structure or sculptural art. Not only does it have responsibilities to the public realm; it is the setting for an enriched way of life, and people are at the centre of the design. Yet architecture is notorious for its gap between real life and pure aesthetics, for its dismissal of nurturing life-enhancing values in favour of aggressive forms that celebrate height, superscale and dominating power. I ascribe this dichotomy to a need for ''feminine'' sensibilities in both the men and women who design buildings, places and environments that must answer the real needs of these complex times.'

'That the built environment suffers from a polarization of female and male values has been evident to me since the 1950s when, as a young design editor, I was asked to write an article for a fashion magazine titled 'Working in a Man's World. ' This dealt with my unusual role as Editor-in -Chief of *Industrial Design*, a professional magazine reaching an audience of predominantly male designers, engineers and corporate executives, dealing with their technical, aesthetic and business concerns. In a field in which a woman was regarded as as 'gifted as a porcupine in public relations' I

was managing (with my co-editor Deborah Allen) to turn the female perspective to natural advantage in interpreting design. Our articles were informed not only with hard facts and real news, but with the insights and attitudes of their ultimate customers, the female purchasers and users of products. This editorial pluralism built a perspective that no other design publication could offer to this special audience.

There was at the time no visible women's movement, no affirmative action, no awareness of equality or complementarity between the sexes. I was presented as something of a pioneer, demonstrating to working women that their female characteristics - their often maligned ''subjectivity'', ''instinctual nurturing qualities'', attention to detail, and insights from humble daily experience - were actual strengths to use as assets in the life of corporations, businesses, design practices, or wherever they worked.

A decade later I moved from the cool insulated editorial room into the hot kitchen of architectural practice. Joining BTA, Benjamin Thompson's new firm in 1966 I fell into another pioneering role: architect without portfolio. My critical, verbal and design skills were applied not to drawing or draughting but to conceptualizing, inventing, and articulating ideas and images. I came to describe myself as an advocate-planner cum urban designer representing an outside view. On any project from the conceptual to schematic design phases my input and critiques tended to represent

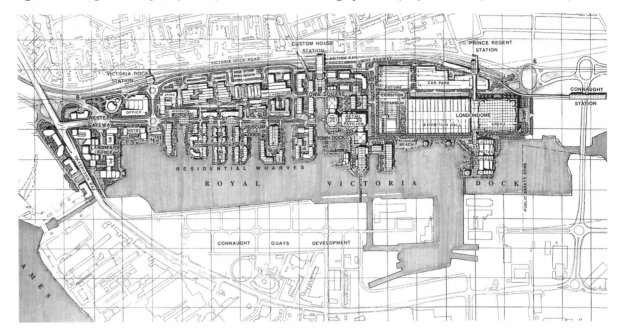

the "other clients" - not usually the owner or builder but
the ultimate occupants (the end user), the unseen citizens
of the world. Starting with the design of dormitory rooms,
campus plans, schools, libraries and auditoriums, the work
progressed to stores, restaurants, town centres, markets and
whole city sectors.

Because BTA's practice was founded on strong ethical
beliefs in the larger social responsibilities of architects, and
on their teamwork, this role not only shaped our planning
but became a central design tool. Ben and I began collaborating on the creation of 'Visions' - strategies for reducing the
negatives of life, for filling voids with better human experience
in more stimulating environments. In the alienating aura of
the Vietnam/Watergate era each job was potentially a little
piece of a better world: a more stimulating school, a more

hospitable city, a better place to shop, gather and socialize
with the community. Our positive vision was expressed in
a collage of words and slide images illustrating ' A New Vision
of the City of Man ', an urban prophesy that became a design
model; we presented it widely in lectures and articles from
1966 onwards through the 1970s.

Our immediate vision was local - saving old Boston market place. Ben had identified and photographed the old crum-
bling market in 1965, and by early 1967 we were articulating
ideas and proposing that the city restore it as a vital contemporary market centre. In a business sense it was a crazy
idea based on pure invention and unrestrained idealism. But
we knew, as travellers to the old city centres of Europe and
Scandinavia, that our ideas had urban validity; we knew simply as citizens - consumers, homemakers and parents in

115

1978-, and a director of the Kaufman International Design Award from 1960-67. She has lectured on Design at Harvard and Yale Universities, the Pratt Institute and Bennington College, Illinois Institute of Technology. Since the late 1960s Jane Thompson has studied human perceptual processes in relation to learning and to environmental experience. She has written about the concepts which underlie the practice's work and its concern for designing urban spaces and uses which encourage human interaction and well-being. She jointly owns, with her husband Ben Thompson, the Harvest Restaurant in Cambridge, Mass., and owns and is managing director of the Landmark Inn complex of three restaurants and wine bar in Boston's Faneuil Hall Marketplace.
Selected articles written by Jane Thompson: 'Very Significant Chair', originally printed in *Harper's Magazine*, 1959. 'the haus of bauhaus reconsidered', *Progressive Architecture*, 1966. 'World of the double win: Male and Female principles in Design ', *The Designer*, 1976. 'Boston's Faneuil Hall', *Urban Design International*, 1979. 'In Search of the Real City', *Space and Society*, 1984.

Above left: Ghiradelli Square, San Francisco, 1983-7. Public square and cafe pavilion. When the old chocolate factory at Ghiradelli Square ceased manufacture, B.T.A was called in to suggest new uses for the building and surrounding area. Happy people with weary feet rest before descending to Fisherman's Wharf.
Below left: The Pavilion at the Old Post Office, Washington D.C., 1981-4. Concept and retail planning.

Articles with Ben
Thompson: 'Let's Make it
Real', *Architectural Record*,
1966. 'The World Around
Us: Toward an Architecture
of Joy and Human
Sensibility ', *Architectural
Record*, 1967. 'A New Vision
of the City of Man',
Architectural Record, 1969.
'The Craft of Design and
the Art of Building', Louis
Sullivan Award Address,
1985.

Above right: Union
Station, Washington
D.C., 1984-8.
Revitalization of the
historic station building
which is still used for its
original purpose.
Below right: Inter
Continental Hotel, Abu
Dhabi, United Arab
Emirates, 1974-82.
Islamic restaurant
design. B.T.A. designed
interiors for a number
of Inter Continental
hotels in Abu Dhabi.
Jane Thompson
undertook extensive
research of Islamic non-
representational art
before making
proposals.

Boston - that a city with such a vital marketplace at its heart
would be a better community for people. Propelled by gut
conviction we planned, designed and pushed numbers to
demonstrate the feasibility of our retail concepts. Ultimately
(it took a decade of high politics) the plans were accepted,
implemented, and put into operation as Faneuil Hall Marketplace, 1967-78.

Larger changes followed in the 1980s - an historic seaport,
new and old city centres, rebuilt commercial cores, water-
fronts around the world - each one in its way an active and
harmonious place bringing people together for personal and
communal enjoyment. In addition to formulating programmes
and articulating concepts (and helping to run an office of up
to one hundred people) my contributions involved retail planning and merchandising, for example in the renovation of
Ghiradelli Square in San Francisco and the revitalization of
Union Station in Washington, D. C. , and mixed use developments such as London's Royal Victoria Docks and Dublin's
Custom House Docks. The most recent project under my
direction is a master plan for New York's Grand Central District in which we are achieving by re-design of paving, planting, lighting, public space and innumerable street details, a
more civilized urban street environment for fifty blocks in
the heart of Manhattan.'

117

Britain   Patricia Tindale

Biography
Born in 1926 in the United
Kingdom. Educated at the
Architectural Association
School of Architecture,
London. Obtained the A. A.
Diploma, 1948. Associate of
the Royal Institute of
British Architects (A. R. I.
B. A.). Registered
architect in the United
Kingdom. Alfred Bossom
fellowship, 1964, to study
housebuilding in the U.S.A.
Patricia Tindale was Chief
Architect at the Department
of the Environment (DOE).
For twenty years she
worked within central
government Ministries and
Departments researching
and developing theories
which were then tested in
built form. Following
retirement in 1986 she
works as a consultant in
private practice. From 1949-
60 she worked for the
Ministry of Education
Development Group in
Cardiff and London on the
design of prototype pre-
fabricated school buildings.
From 1961-72 she worked
with the Ministry of
Housing and Local
Government Research and
Development Group on the
design and construction of
prototype housing. The
research results were
published by Her Majesty's
Stationery Office, official
publisher for the
government, in the form of
'Bulletins'. From 1972-74
Head of Building
Regulations Professional
Division at the Department
of the Environment. Head
of the Housing
Development Directorate,
1974-80. Director of the
Central Unit of the Built
Environment, 1981. Chief
Architect of the Department
of the Environment
responsible for architectural
policy, 1982-6. Chair of the
sponsoring committee of
the Housing Design awards.
Assessor for the
Times/RIBA/Gulbenkian
Community Enterprise
Scheme. Member of RIBA's
Education and Professional

'The most exciting opportunity for an architect, who like me, qualified in the late 1940s, was to work on one of the post-war building programmes for schools, housing or hospitals,' comments Patricia Tindale, retired Chief Architect of the Department of the Environment and former holder of the highest position in central government open to an architect. 'After years of destruction, and in the euphoria of victory, people were determined to create a new Britain and to have the buildings that would go with it.'

'The key word was 'programme' and the underlying idea was that buildings would be commissioned in parallel and not just one at a time. This meant that much more thought could be put into user research and technical development. The Ministry of Education Development Group in which I worked, was the first set up in a central government department for architects to work with educationalists, administrators and the construction industry. Our task was to produce and publish design information for various types of schools as an aid for the architects of individual buildings. We also developed systems of construction using kits of component parts and built first- off projects, the aim being to enable buildings to be built quickly at a time when labour and materials were scarce.'

'I spent a happy decade at the Ministry of Education before transferring to the Ministry of Housing and Local Government where a similar group was being set up. Here the task was much more difficult. Some of the post-war enthusiasm had evaporated and housing, then as now, is much more subject to political vagaries at all levels than other public buildings. Nevertheless a series of Design Bulletins on user requirements emerged based on discussions with people at

home and other research. Kit-of-parts systems were developed and prototype schemes were built.'

'We always worked in democratic teams designing buildings, but I feel I have the greatest claim to a secondary grammar school at Arnold in Nottinghamshire; the development of the 5M system of construction based on earlier work for a school at Belper in Derbyshire; and the development of a lightweight party wall system.'

'In 1971 a three month course at the Manchester Business School proved to be a watershed in my professional life because I came to see that my future would not necessarily lie in work centred on live building projects. In 1972 I became head of the Department of the Environment's Building Regulations Professional Division. The job was more enthralling than it might at first appear - how to set requirements which would ensure the health and safety of people in buildings while leaving the maximum freedom for architects and engineers to design. My two short years in this post saw two exciting new ventures; the introduction of national requirements for energy conservation following the first oil crisis, and the first steps towards European integration in building regulations and standards.'

'I then returned to housing as head of the Housing Development Directorate until its disbandment in 1980. The advent of the Conservative administration in 1979 led to a sea change in government policy towards building. The large scale public programmes were swept away and detailed control removed in favour of selective action to secure that clients, both public and private, realized that it was their responsibility to commission good architecture. For example the National Housebuilding Council became joint spon-

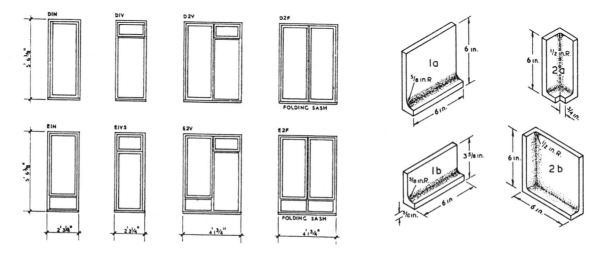

Development Committee.
Selected work:
Grammar school at Arnold,
Nottinghamshire. School at
Belper, Derbyshire.
Development of the 5M
construction system and
lightweight party wall
construction system.
Publications:
*Ministry of Education
Building Bulletin 17*,
HMSO, 1960. *Housebuilding
in the U.S.A.*, HMSO, 1965.
*Designing a low-rise housing
system*, Ministry of Housing
and Local Government Design
Bulletin 18, HMSO, 1970.

Experimental secondary
school at Arnold,
Nottinghamshire, 1958.
Ministry of Education
Building Development
Group. The school was
the sixth secondary
school undertaken by
the development group
of architects. It
embodies some unusual
features both in the plan
and in the new system
of construction
developed.

Below: Detail of the 5M
structural system
designed by the
Ministry of Housing and
Local Government
Development Group in
the 1960s.

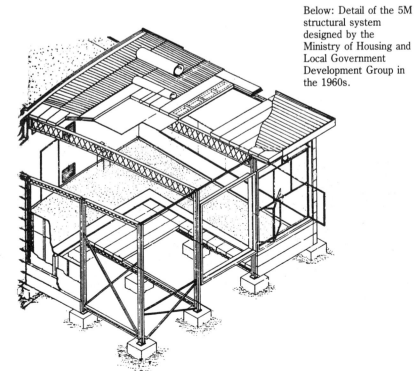

sor, with the Department of the Environment and the Royal
Institute of British Architects, of Housing Design Awards.
Architectural competitions where the client made the final
choice of the scheme to be built were encouraged - many
sponsored by the Government's own Property Services
Agency. The Department of the Environment actively supported the R.I.B.A.'s Festival of Architecture in two ways:
by producing a film *More than just a Road*, aimed at achieving better housing development layouts, and a book *Art for
Architecture*. As Chief Architect at the Department of the
Environment I was fortunate to see many of these new policies being developed and implemented.'

Far left: Standardized
windows - the fore
runner to further
standardized
components. Ministry of
Works, 1944, and
standard clay floor tiles,
1946.

USA   Susana Torre

Susana Torre.

Biography
Born 1944 in Puan,
Argentina. Resident in the
USA since 1968. Educated
at the University of Buenos
Aires, 1964-7, receiving an
Architecture degree in 1967.
Further studies at the
Instituto Superior de
Planeamiento Urbano at the
University of Buenos Aires
in 1967. Post graduate
studies at Columbia
University, New York, 1968-
9, on a fellowship from the
University of Buenos Aires.
Principal of Susana Torre
and Associates, 1990-. Prior
to this President of Susana
Torre Raymond Beeler and
Associates, 1988-9, and
Partner in Wank Adams
Slavin Associates, New
York, 1985-7. Principal of
the Architectural Studio,
New York, 1978-84. Susana
Torre's built work over the
last decade includes urban
design, public buildings, and
house, office and
institutional building
renovations. Academic
appointments have included
visiting critic and adjunct
Professor of Architecture at
Columbia University, New
York; Yale University;
Cooper Union, New York;
Carnegie Mellon and
Syracuse University, New
York from 1973 - 1980.
Associate Professor of
Architecture at New Jersey
Institute of Technology,
1977-8. Director,
Architecture Programme,
Barnard College, 1982-5.
Associate Professor of
Architecture, Columbia

Susana Torre is an Argentinian born and trained architect who has lived and worked in New York since 1968, when she arrived on a fellowship to study at Columbia University. Since the early 1980s she has combined the teaching and study of architecture with the running of a successful practice.

While still a student in Argentina, she established the first Architecture and Design department in a Latin American museum for the city of La Plata. Her own house, which she built when she was 18 years old, employed the simple, bold forms which characterize her recent work.

In New York, during the 1970s, she researched the history of modern architecture and the planning of new towns at the Museum of Modern Art and the Institute for Architecture and Urban Studies. At the same time she initiated the design curriculum for the State University of New York at old Westbury.

In 1978 she started her own practice, the Architectural Studio, based in central New York. It received immediate recognition with the publication of her designs for 'Law Offices'.

She is widely regarded as a major figure in the field of architectural education, and has drawn to her a group of younger architects with whom she collaborated on a number of successful competitions and exhibitions. The group's 1986 exhibition, 'Room in the City', was a series of new ideas and design proposals tackling the problem of minimum housing standards. In 1987 she organized an important conference on the neglected subject of Hispanic architecture in the United States, and a decade earlier brought together a group of writers to jointly produce a book, *Women in American Architecture: a historic and contemporary perspective* - a subject rarely touched upon at that time.

Although her 1980s architectural commissions have been for institutional and residential buildings, her projects range from furniture design to suggestions for an American city of the future. In 1985 she joined the group of famous architects commissioned to design public buildings in Columbus, Indiana, and was asked to design Fire Station Number 5, completed in 1987.

The visual variety in her buildings can be attributed to her avowed commitment to regional expression in the use of local building materials and techniques.

In 1980 Torre wrote about her approach to architecture in the catalogue of the Venice Biennale's first international exhibition of architecture. She wrote on the theme of the exhibition, 'The Presence of the Past.'

'I find myself as "He" finds himself in Kafka's parable, staking my ground, clashing in either direction with two powerful forces. The past does not pull me back but presses forward, and it is, contrary to what one would expect, the future which drives me back into the past. In the interval between past and future, my presence causes the forces to deflect from their original direction. The resulting diagonal force, whose origin is the clash between past and future, but whose end is unknown, marks the place where my own work finds its meaning and direction.'

Graduate School of Architecture, Planning and Preservation, New York, 1981-. Ms Torre has acted as consultant to Eastern Airlines, Partners for Liveable Spaces, Washington, DC. , the Ivory Coast Government Mission to the United Nations, the Cultural Council Foundation, New York, and the United States Department of Commerce, Washington, DC. She has received seven fellowships and awards, including four from the National Endowment for the Arts over the period 1967-1986. Susana Torre is editor and co-author of 'Women in American Architecture: a Historic and Contemporary perspective ', 1977, and co-editor of 'Making room: Women in Architecture', 1981. She has written many articles on architecture, and given over seventy public lectures in Canada, Spain, Portugal, and South America, as well as in the USA. Her work has been exhibited in 35 group shows at major museums and galleries and she has been curator of two travelling architectural exhibitions. She is a Board member of Architects for Social Responsibility and on the Board of Directors of the Architectural League of New York, 1986-7. She has also been a judge on 28 advisory boards for organizations such as the American Institute of Architects and the National Endowment for the Arts.

Left: Fire station Five, Columbus Indiana. Exterior. The two vertical towers contain a stair-cum-fireman's pole and a hose drying tower. They are reminiscent of local Indiana farm silos.

Right Clark House, Southampton, New York. Exterior elevation. Renovation of a 1917, shingle clad carriage house.

Private residence, Amangansett, New York. Garden elevation. 'I think of this house as a sun porch attached to a tower', says Torre, who designed the house to follow the path of the sun. The upper level dining room has views over the garden to the ocean.

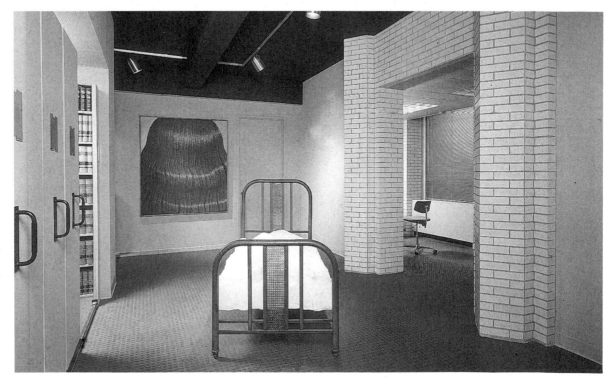

Law Offices, New York City, 1975. Sculpture gallery with library to the right and secretaries to the left. ' Sleeping figure' by George Segal. This scheme, designed for the offices of a prominent international lawyer and collector of surrealist art, established Torre's reputation as a designer.

Exercise room, Fire
station Five.

Below: Civic Centre
Master Plan, City of
Hemet, California.
Aerial view. Camphor
trees cut across the city
grid, lining a proposed
walk along old railroad
tracks.

123

Anne Griswold Tyng

Biography
Educated at Radcliffe
College, Harvard University,
BA, 1938-42. Attended
Smith Graduate school of
Architecture and Landscape
Architecture, 1941-2, and
Harvard Graduate School of
Design, 1942-44, obtaining a
Masters degree in
Architecture. Received a
doctorate from the
University of Pennsylvania
in 1975. Registered as an
architect in Pennsylvania
and with the National
Council of Architects
Registration Boards in 1949.
Elected Fellow of the
American Institute of
Architects and Associate of
the National Academy of
Design in 1975. Granted two
fellowships by the Graham
Foundation for Advanced
study in the Fine Arts in
1963 and 1979.
Anne Griswold Tyng
collaborated with Louis
Kahn in Philadelphia during
the 1950s and 60s and is
jointly responsible for the
development of many of his
theories about architecture.
Until recently, her name
has been overshadowed by
his in the outside world.
Griswold Tyng's work in
1944-5 in New York
included interiors and
furniture for Knoll
Associates Planning Unit. In
the late forties it included
design and construction of
prefabricated steel houses
and a project for a solar
house. From 1945-1973 she
worked in, or as consultant
to, Louis Kahn's office on a
wide range of buildings and
planning proposals including
a four year period from
1949-53 on Philadelphia's
Psychiatric Hospital. She
designed Yale University's
Art Gallery from 1951-3,
public housing between
1952 and 1962 at Mill Creek
in Philadelphia, and four
private houses between
1951 and 1961. In addition
there were planning studies
for areas in Philadelphia,
and development of theories
on 'servant spaces' and the
use of geometric forms.

Anne Griswold Tyng has always believed that the bedrock of good architecture lies in theoretical research.

She has developed theories which encompass three dimensional geometry, visual perception, psychology, the mathematics of the Fibonacci series and Platonic solids, together with an understanding of the effects of scale. The all-inclusive nature of her theories drew initially upon the geodesic work of Buckminster Fuller in the fifties, and her long term collaboration with Louis Kahn. During the twenty years that she either worked with Kahn or was consultant to his office she designed a number of influential buildings including Yale University's Art Gallery at New Haven, Connecticut, completed in 1953. This building, with its tetrahedral reinforced concrete ceiling system and exposed mechanical services, utilizes the 'servant spaces' theory which was developing in Kahn's office at the time, in which a spatial and psychological relationship can be shown between different elements of the design.

New theories continued to develop in the 1960s and 1970s. She put considerable thought into geometric research, discovering a new super Pythagorean theorem in which she documented new three dimensional Divine Proportion configurations. A theory of human scale and its extension to the man-made environment followed, together with a study of London squares which developed into certain 'principles of scale'. This work, seen with hindsight, fits neatly into current day research undertaken by mathematicians and scientists to develop the much favoured 'Chaos' theory.

While she researched, lectured, taught and wrote, Griswold Tyng also built. With Kahn's office she was closely involved with two highly regarded buildings, a Jewish Community centre at Trenton, New Jersey in 1959, and the design of dormitories at Bryn Mawr College, Philadelphia in 1965.

In 1967, working independently, she designed an award winning roof addition to her own house in Philadelphia and during the next decade experimented with prototypes for low budget energy efficient solar and wind powered houses.

Anne Griswold Tyng's buildings are infused with her love for, and exciting use of geometric spaces and her deep knowledge of the technology - often quite simple - required to achieve dramatic design solutions.

Her 1953 holiday house, with its dramatic and clearly geometric shape, was the first of its kind to be built. Her drawings for a house to be built by the owner in four stages on Mount Desert Island, Maine, 1978-88, carry on this interest more than a quarter of a century later and show a remarkable consistency throughout a long career.

Waverly Street roof addition, Philadelphia, 1967. Studio with bed loft.

The latter theory was developed between 1953 and 1957 into a project for the Universal Atlas Cement Company called 'Tomorrow's City Hall ', and her interest in the relevance of geometrical relationships has remained a mainstay of her practical and theoretical work. In addition to her work with Kahn, Anne Griswold Tyng designed and built on her own account for clients. Her 1953 addition to a farmhouse near Cambridge, Maryland received an Honour Award from the Philadelphia Chapter of the A. I. A. for its ingenious structural system and her unusual roof level development of a Philadelphia town house in 1967 received critical acclaim. In 1980 she developed a prototype sprayed plastic building for a firm of builders and constructed a vacation home for a member of the firm, using solar and wind power. In the late 1980s she designed two low budget houses, one of them to be built by the owner himself, and a new exhibition pavilion for Chestnut Hill Academy of Art.
Tyng has taught at Carnegie Mellon University, Cooper

Union, New York, the University of Texas at Austin, Pennselaer Polytechnic Institute, Pratt Institute, and the University of Pennsylvania, where she is an Adjunct Associate Professor. During the last 17 years she has been invited to lecture at national institutions and schools of Architecture throughout America and in England, Canada, and at Xian University in China. She has written for a large number of publications over the last 30 years and her latest contribution, on recurring cycles in the history of architecture, was published in 1989. Her work has been included in 15 exhibitions since 1960 including *That Exceptional One: Women in American Architecture 1888-1988*, a travelling exhibition mounted by the A.I.A. , *Unbuilt and Built Architecture by Women*, Philadelphia, 1988, and *Austin Women Architects*, Texas, 1988. She has received two awards from the New York Chapter of the A.I.A. for research work on *The Divine Proportion in the Platonic Solids*, 1964, and for a study of London Squares, 1983. She was invited to speak at the First World Congress of Women Architects in Iran, 1976, at the XIII World Congress of Architects, Mexico City, 1978, and at Aspen International Design Conference, 1980. Anne Griswold Tyng is the subject of four video films made between 1972 and 1977 about her teaching and research. Her work is listed in the *Dictionary of International Biography*, the *World Who's Who of Women*, *World Who's Who of Intellectuals*, *Who's Who of America*, *Who's Who of American Women*, *Who's Who in the World* and *Macmillan's Encyclopaedia of Architects*.

Walworth Tyng house, Cambridge, Maryland, 1953. The first triangulated space frame structure used for living in.

Australia

Christine Vadasz

Christine Vadasz

Biography
Born in Budapest, Hungary,
in 1946, moved to Australia
in 1949. Educated at the
University of Adelaide,
South Australia, Bachelor of
Architecture, 1970.
Associate of the Royal
Australian Institute of
Architects.
Christine Vadasz is director
of Christine Vadasz
Architects, Byron Bay, New
South Wales, which she
started in 1974. She worked
for Bill Lucas in Sydney,
1970-73. She was winner of
the President's award by
the Royal Australian
Institute of Architects in
1984. She taught at Sydney
University in 1985 and at
the architecture school of
the Institute of Technology
in Hobart, Tasmania, 1986.
In 1987 she was a guest
speaker at the Biennial
Oceanic Architectural
Education Congress in
Hobart and lectured on
tourist development in
remote and sensitive sites
at a conference held by the
R. A.I.A. in Tasmania,
1989.
Selected work:
Housing:3-4 rural and
suburban single dwellings
per year since 1977. 'Old
Bakery' shopping complex,
Byron Bay, New South
Wales, 1980. 'Beachfront'
tourist accomodation, Byron
Bay, New South Wales,
1981. Oncology clinic and
garden for New South
Wales Health Department,
Lismore, New South Wales,
1986. Bedarra Bay resort
for Australian Airlines,
Bedarra Island, North

In 1984 Christine Vadasz found herself winner of the President of the Royal Australian Institute of Architects award in recognition of her work in developing a regional approach to architecture. Her subtle and innovative designs for the tourist industry in Australia have won her repeat commissions from Australian Airlines. Meanwhile her fame has spread to Java where she has been asked to develop a resort on the West coast.

'My heart responds to the sub-tropical environment of Eastern Australia where I live,' says Vadasz, a resident of Byron Bay, New South Wales. 'The heavy rainfall of one season followed by the drought of the next, and the magnificent rainforest remnants and dwindling natural habitats such as the coastal wetlands, encourage me to respect nature, landforms and the movement of water.'

'However I was born in Central Europe, although I left Budapest at three years of age and came to Australia. Like so many migrant children in a new world I was brought up and nutured in Central European traditions. This taught me to respect art, the artisan and craftsmanship far more than my teachers or colleagues at university or in the architectural profession. An Hungarian upbringing teaches you to enjoy life whilst you can and this has helped me to bring fun and enjoyment into my architecture. I allow my sense of design to flow from my emotions and reactions to nature around me rather than from the up-tight rationales and the forced logic of much architecture.'

'When I travelled in Asia I was deeply influenced by traditional design techniques which come to grips with climate and the environment, no matter how harsh. What you find - whether in the Zen approach in Japan or the joyous Hindu philosophy of the Balinese culture - is an architecture which seeks to accomodate nature rather than to dominate it.'

'In the late sixties I worked, as a student, in I. M. Pei's office in New York and learnt a great deal, but when I left I knew I would never again want to work in a large office. On graduation from Adelaide University in 1970 I worked for an ''alternative'' architect in Sydney, Bill Lucas, and this period taught me that a creative environment must be friendly, non-sexist and preferably homely.'

'After this I set out to build my own distinctive design practice which would embody my attitudes to work and relaxation. Numbers are limited to those who can fit around the coffee table for morning tea and we all consciously attempt to keep too strongly commercial attitudes at bay whilst still working with developers and private clients. If there is a lot of work we work hard. If there is a lull we go surfing'.

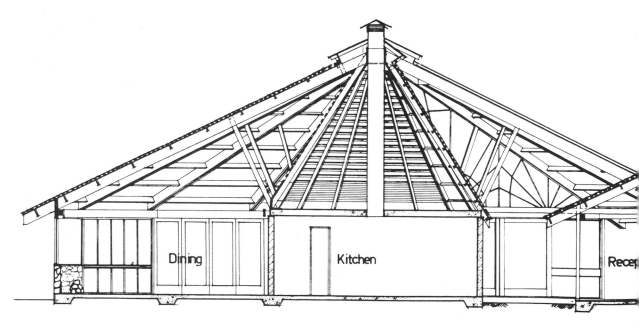

Dining   Kitchen   Recep

Queensland, 1986. Wheel resort for disabled tourists, Byron Bay, New South Wales, 1986. Hideaway resort for Australian Airlines, Bedarra Island, North Queensland, 1987. New amenities for Currumbin Bird Sanctuary for the National Trust of Queensland, Currumbin, Queensland, 1988.
Awards:
Duncan's Award for Design Excellence in Timber for Bedarra Bay resort, Bedarra Island, North Queensland, 1987.
Queensland Chapter of the R.A.I.A. Awards: Non residential award for Hideaway Resort, Bedarra Island, North Queensland, 1988. Commendation 'Residential Award 1988' for the Hoffman residence, Goondiwindi, Queensland. Christine Vadasz's work has been exhibited at *Australia Built*, 1985-6, and at the PAM-SIA Commonwealth Association of Architects Conference in Kuala Lumpur, Malaysia, 1989.

Above: Bedarra Bay resort. Guest rooms.

Right: Bedarra Bay resort. Bar in the main complex.

Far left: Bedarra Bay resort, Bedarra Island, North Queensland, 1986.

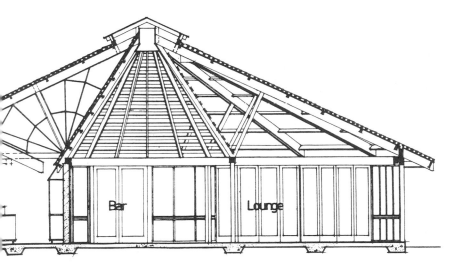

127

Thorpe residence.
Outside dining area.

Hoffman residence.

Bedarra Hideaway
resort. Exterior of the
main complex.

Bedarra Hideaway
resort, Bedarra Island,
North Queensland,
1987. Guest room on
the beach.

Sweden

Maud Vretblad

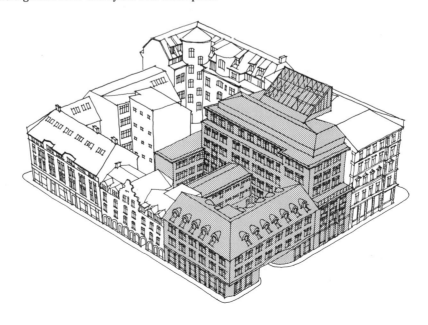

Maud Vretblad.

Biography
Born in 1942. Educated at the Royal Institute of Technology, Stockholm obtaining a degree in Architecture, 1970. Further studies in social science, 1972-3, and at the Royal Academy of Fine Arts School of Architecture in 1974. Member of SAR, the National Association of Swedish Architects. Associate of Berg Arkitektkontor AB, Stockholm. Built work includes factory construction and re-development, industrial workshops, corporate offices, and city renewal in central Stockholm, and includes the following buildings: Albin Marin Yacht manufacturing plant, Kristinehamn, Sweden, 1975. Billerud Uddeholm papermill and office, Skoghall, Sweden, 1976. Iggesund papermill, Iggesund, Sweden, 1977. Holmens Bruk mineral wool plant, Vrena, Sweden, 1978. Offices for the Design division of Saab-Scania, Sodertalje, Sweden, 1979. Maintenance workshop, Iggesund papermill, Iggesund, Sweden, 1982. Headquarters for Swedish Farmers Meat Marketing Association, Stockholm, Sweden, 1982. Medical Centre for Saab-Scania, Sodertalje, Sweden, 1985. Sundbyberg District Heating Plant renovation manual, Sundbyberg, Sweden, 1984.

Maud Vretblad's work with Berg AB has taken her directly to the heart of Swedish manufacturing. In her chosen field of planning, design and building for industry she has faced the complexities of Sweden's paper industry and undertaken three separate projects for the motor vehicle company, Saab-Scania.

In the late 1980s the accent partly shifted to city regeneration and development in central Stockholm, together with the construction of headquarters for Linjeflyg, Sweden's domestic airline.

The Linjeflyg design followed an internal training project which Berg AB ran in-house in 1984 when members of the firm were called upon to design offices following current philosophies about office design, namely the 'Economic', 'Technical', 'Architectural' and 'Individual' viewpoints. It was the latter, with its interest in the welfare of the person at work, which interested Maud Vretblad.

She states, 'My main consideration has always been the people who work in the building or those who are to use it. Even with industrial premises where the process itself has been of paramount importance my main concern has been how the occupants will experience the building. I have therefore always worked upon projects from the inside outwards, starting from the individual's need to function in the company of others.'

At Linjeflyg's headquarters at Arlanda airport outside Stockholm, completed in 1988, the square building is designed around a ground floor courtyard with a computer hall beneath. The main entrance is at one corner of the square with the block skewed at forty five degrees to the access road. The internal courtyard is far more than a well designed circulation space. People sit at tables, relax and eat under a glazed roof which offers not only protection from the normal rigours of the Swedish climate but - as important in an airport environment - reduced noise levels. Most of the offices are placed along the edge of the building and therefore have views of the Arlanda woods in the distance. For those few with offices facing on to the internal courtyard, considerable care has been taken to relate to the world beyond through the use of pivoting windows which steal reflections of sky and draw down natural light from the large glazed roof over the courtyard.

In her regeneration and development of the Bryggmastaren Complex in central Stockholm, completed in 1986, Maud Vretblad shows consummate skill in solving the conflicting requirements of the preservation of city centre buildings and increasing the density of development in a manner acceptable to both client and public. More than seventy five per cent of existing street facades have been retained through rehabilitation of the buildings, and where new ones have replaced old, great care has been taken to respect the scale of the street.

Access to offices in the middle of the development, and to the successful open air cafe in the central courtyard, is available to the public from all four surrounding streets.

The Bryggmastaren
Complex. Complete
renovation, including
substantial new
construction, of a central
area of Stockholm,
completed 1986. Braviken
papermill development plan,
Norrkoping, Sweden, 1988.
Thermo-mechanical pulpmill
for Braviken papermill,
Norrkoping, Sweden, 1988.
Linjeflyg headquarters,
(Swedish domestic airline),
Stockholm Arlanda,
Sweden, 1988. Saab-Scania
VIP restaurants, Sodertalje,
Sweden, 1989. Holmens
Bruk power plant,
Norrkoping, Sweden. Under
construction. Conversion of
a former tobacco warehouse
into offices, restaurants, and
boutiques for Procordia,
Stockholm, Sweden. Under
construction.

Above: Bryggmastaren complex. Internal courtyard.
Right: Bryggmastaren complex. New buildings along
Malargatan.

Far left: Bryggmastaren complex, Stockholm, 1986.
Diagram showing the renovated block. Darker areas are
new building.

Below: Linjeflyg Headquarters, Arlanda airport, Stockholm, 1988. Plan
Right: Linjeflyg Headquarters. Internal covered courtyard.
Below right: Linjeflyg Headquarters. View from First floor corner balcony.

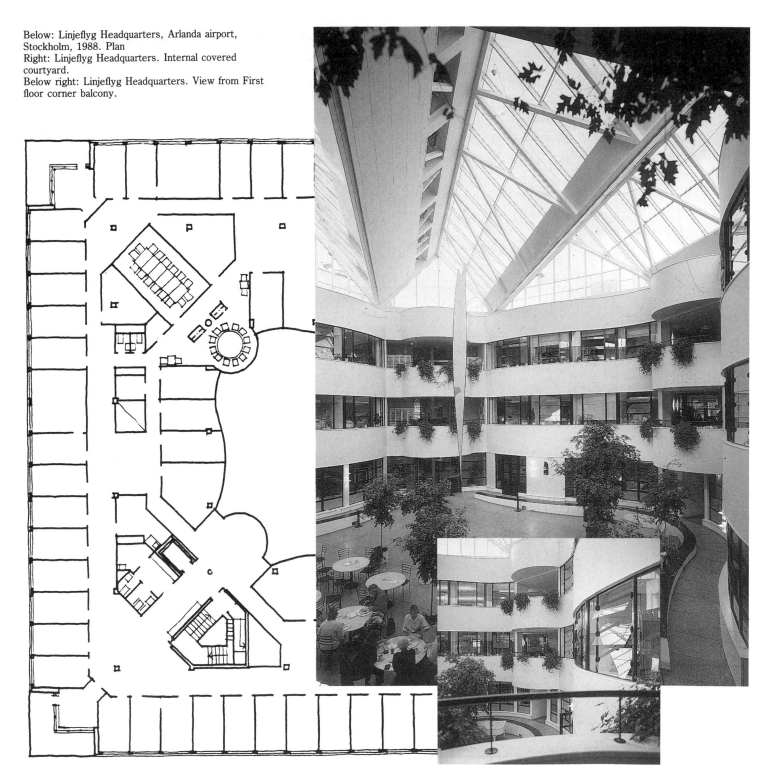

Saab-Scania conference
room, Sodertalje,
Sweden, 1989.

Albin Marin Yacht
factory, Kristinehamn,
1975.

USA — Beverly Willis

Beverly Willis

Biography
Born in 1928 in the USA. Educated at the University of Hawaii, Honolulu, B. A. 1954. Awarded an honorary doctorship from Mount Holyoke College in 1982. Fellow of the American Institute of Architects, 1980. Beverly Willis is design principal of her own firm, which is known as Beverly Willis, Architect. The practice, started in 1966, has two offices, one on the West coast of the United States in San Francisco, the second, which opened in 1988, on the East coast in Stockbridge, Massachusetts. The practice has concentrated on two fields - the performing arts and housing, which ranges from individual houses to mass housing for the US army. In recent years, after completion of the highly praised San Francisco ballet building in the centre of the city in 1984, Ms Willis has been offered further theatre complexes and it is these which are now the major focus of the firm. From 1954-1966 Beverly Willis worked as an artist and designer on a range of commissions. These included a wood sculpture for United Airlines in Honolulu, Hawaii, a series of geometric abstractions in oils for the Honolulu Art Gallery museum, and a fresco for the United Chinese Society in Honolulu. She has also designed furniture which was exhibited at the

Beverly Willis believes firmly that worthwhile design is tied intrinsically to its era. She comments, 'The functional, social and economic credos of the times shape the architect's design idea. The architect's knowledge and experience is formed by today's scientific and technological discoveries and social mores. My design process is an attempt to achieve balance between the traditional and the new. To me this is important because I believe that inhumane architecture results when balance is lost.'

Nowadays most of Beverly Willis' work is the design of buildings for the visual and performing arts. She commutes between San Francisco, where she started her firm, Beverly Willis, Architect, in 1966, and her office outside New York which was opened in 1988.

Her career began most unusually. After studying for two years to be an engineer she left university and pursued her interests in writing, printing and drawing. In 1952 she returned to further study and took an arts degree at the University of Hawaii after studying painting, lithography, ceramics and photography.

During this period she started a crafts business in Hawaii, the Willis Workshop, and after graduation was commissioned to design and produce the sculpture, artifacts and furniture which were integrated with a traditional Hawaiian thatched building - complete with tapa cloth walls - to become the Shell Bar cocktail lounge which was used regularly on the set of the television series *Hawaii Five-O*.

She was then commissioned by the admiral in charge of the Pacific armed forces to re-design the interior of his headquarters. More than satisfied with what he found, he recommended her for contracts to design officer's clubs, with responsibility for all architectural aspects, engineering, contracting and furnishing.

By 1960 the Willis Workshop had become Willis and Associates, Inc. and Beverly Willis had realized that certain types of construction were unlikely to be built on Hawaii. So she moved her practice to San Francisco in 1960 and began working on small scale housing and theatre renovation projects, followed at the end of the decade by larger scale work.

One of her first major projects was the renovation of three nineteenth century buildings in Union Street, San Francisco, in 1963. By retaining the exteriors, but changing from residential to commercial use, she set the style for regeneration of the Union Street commercial district. It was one of the first projects of its kind and its great success was recognised throughout the United States. Soon afterwards she restored buildings in Jackson Square, San Francisco, and the rejuvenation of this area foreshadowed national efforts to restore old buildings in city centres.

National recognition came to Beverly Willis with her 1972 conversion of Vine Terrace apartments, renamed Nob Hill condominiums.

In the late 1970s her work focused increasingly on visual and performing arts buildings and she was able to merge her skills in art, architecture and engineering.

Her arts buildings are designed to support the performer through sensitive design of space, light, and good acoustic and environmental control. Her best-known performing arts building is for the San Francisco Ballet in the civic centre, completed in 1984. She also restored the Glide memorial multi-purpose auditorium and community centre in San Francisco, 1971, the Oakland Ensemble theatre, California, 1985, and the Berkshire Festival theatre, one of the oldest off-Broadway summer theatres in the United States, 1989–.

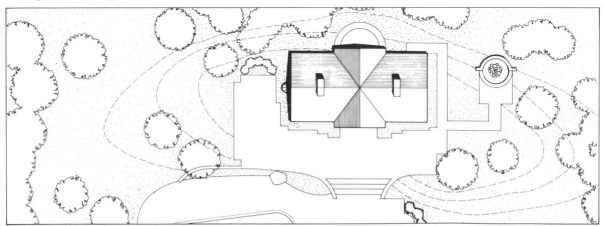

Cooper-Hewitt museum in New York, 1988, at the San Francisco garden show, contract design centre, San Francisco, and the Topher Delaney outdoor chair show in Sausalito, California. In 1980 she came first in an international competition for the design and development of a billion dollar mixed use development in central San Francisco at Yerba Buena Gardens. This was developed from 1980-3 into a master plan for the twenty four acre site and includes a visual arts centre, new home for the San Francisco museum of modern art, a Marriott hotel and 1.5 million square feet of office space. *Selected built work includes*: Award winning eleven store shopping complex at Union Street, San Francisco, California, 1963. Conversion of the Glide memorial multi-purpose auditorium in central San Francisco, 1971. Vine Terrace appartments, renamed Nob Hill Court condominiums, San Francisco, 1972. 525 apartments and town houses for 11,500 members of the U.S. Engineers Corps at Aliamano Valley Community in Honolulu, Hawaii, 1976. River Run vineyard residence at St. Helena, California, 1984. Margaret S. Hayward playground building for the City of San Francisco Department of Parks and Recreation, San Francisco, 1979. San Francisco Ballet Association building for the San Francisco Ballet, in the civic centre performing arts complex, San Francisco, 1984. Oakland ensemble theatre at the Alice Arts Centre, Oakland, California, 1985. Pool house and centre for entertaining at Yountville, California, 1988. Current theatre projects include the renovation of the Berkshire theatre festival theatres, studios, residences and teaching facilities complex, and development of the Jacob's Pillow 340 acre dance centre. Also under way are a health centre for the

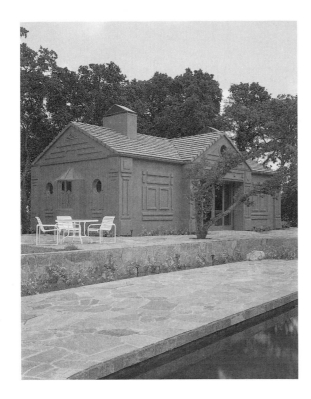

Above left: Pool house, Yountville. Exterior showing the pool.
Above: Pool house, Yountville. Exterior with front and rear doors opened wide.

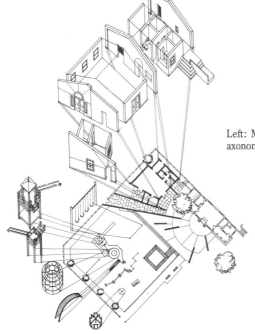

Left: Margaret S. Hayward Playground building. Exploded axonometric and plan.

Far left: Pool house, Yountville, California, 1988. Site Plan.

135

Yerba Buena Gardens district of San Francisco and master plan for a wildlife safari park in Winston, Oregon.

In 1980 Beverly Willis was president of the California council of the A.I.A. and in 1969 was awarded the Phoebe Hearst gold medal award for distinguished service to San Francisco. She attended the United Nations conference on settlements, 'Habitat', in 1976 as the US government's representative.

Awards:

A. I. A Bay area award for Union Street store development, San Francisco, California, 1967. Governor of California's exceptional distinction award for environmental design for Union Street store development, San Francisco, 1967. A.I.A. award of merit for the Vine Terrace apartments, San Francisco, 1976. Gold nugget grand and merit awards from *Builder* magazine and the Pacific coast builders conference for the Margaret S. Hayward playground building, San Francisco, 1983. California council of the A.I.A. merit award for the Margaret S. Hayward playground building, San Francisco, 1984. National Association of Home Builders merit award for River Run residence, St. Helena, California, 1985.

Above: Margaret S. Hayward Playground building, San Francisco, 1979. Exterior.

Right: San Francisco Ballet Building.

San Francisco Ballet
Building. Rehearsal
studio.

San Francisco Ballet
Building, San Francisco,
1984. Exterior showing
its relationship to the
Civic Centre.

Britain   Georgie Wolton

Georgie Wolton

Biography
Born in 1934. Educated at
the Architectural
Association School of
Architecture, London, 1955-
60, obtaining A.A. Diploma,
1960. Member of the Royal
Institute of British
Architects.
Georgie Wolton runs her
own practice in London as a
one woman band. Her great
skill as a landscape architect
is recognised by Richard
Rogers, with whom she has
worked on a number of
projects since 1971. Her
own buildings highlight the
relationship of landscape to
building. She has been a
visiting critic at the Bartlett
and A.A. schools of
architecture, London.
Selected work:
Conversion of house in
London, 1963-4.
Landscaping for housing
association, Blackheath,
London, 1966.
Reconstruction of an 18th
century garden at Ledston
Hall, Yorkshire, 1967.
Fieldhouse, Surrey, 1968.
Cliff Road artists studios,
London, 1969. Landscaping
of house by Richard Rogers
in Wimbledon, 1971. Cliff
Road Studios, second block,
London, 1971-2. House
extension, London, 1972.
Studio, London, 1973.
Courtyard garden,
Hampshire, 1974. House
studio and garden, London,
1975-6. Garden for offices of
Piano & Rogers, London,
1979. Barn conversion and
garden, Gloucestershire,
1979-80. Garden

'My approach to architecture has parallels with seventeenth century landscapes in England, with their axial layouts and geometric parterres, which developed into the episodic and serpentine layouts of the eighteenth century,' states Georgie Wolton. 'It is this period of transition, the cusp between the classical and romantic, which has long been my main preoccupation in both architecture and landscape.'

Georgie Wolton, whose work has moved increasingly towards landscape architecture as her career has progressed, works on her own in a studio attached to the house she built in central London in the 1970s. She does not have a large output of work, but what she does is exquisite.

In 1962 she helped set up Team 4 with Richard Rogers, and Wendy and Norman Foster but soon left because she preferred to work alone. This hermit-like existence, which has been pursued for twenty five years, she regards as a privilege, and it has enabled her to see every aspect of a project through from beginning to end. It is however, not without danger.

'I am acutely aware of the pitfalls of private practice. The law in England makes architects liable for almost any defect, making the cost of professional indemnity insurance prohibitive to a small practice,' she comments.

'Over the years my work has become less geometrical and symmetrical. I used to believe that buildings should be classical in character and have just one right proportion. Fieldhouse, and the two studio blocks at Cliff Road, London, both express this. I still consider that formality has the great advantage of creating calm, but it can inhibit the design of space and surfaces. Nowadays I try to relate the interior space and exterior landscape of a building almost to the point where the garden becomes dominant.'

'In landscape, like William Kent, I've "leapt o'er the fence and seen that all nature was a garden", but I still want to impose an architectural order on what many people in England regard as a horticultural envelope surrounding a house.'

This sense of architectural order, coupled with a keen plantsman's knowledge, has made her a firm favourite with the Richard Rogers Partnership which, over many years, has used her to design outdoor spaces for its schemes. At Thames Wharf, in West London, where the partnership has its offices, she has designed for all three stages of development, 1986-9, and for the partners previous offices and private homes.

reconstruction, London, 1982. Landscaping for Pluto Press, London, 1982. Riverfront landscaping of office development, known as Thames Wharf, for Richard Rogers Partnership, 1986. Roof garden, London, 1984. Landscaping for housing development at Lloyds Wharf, London, 1985. Garden reconstruction, London 1985-7. House extension and creation of hillside garden, Gloucestershire, 1985-6. Second stage landscaping for Thames Wharf for Richard Rogers Partnership, 1986. Landscaping at Dock Manager's office, Surrey Docks, London, 1987. Planting for river cafe at Thames Wharf, London, 1988. Herb garden, Gloucester, 1988. Project for the Arno riverbank, Florence, with Richard Rogers Partnership, 1989. Third stage landscaping at Thames Wharf, London, 1989. Georgic Wolton's work has been exhibited in the R. I. B. A's 1985 exhibition *Women Architects, Their work*.

Left:Cliff Road Artists Studios, London, 1969. Southern light diffused through glass block windows.

Below: Thames Wharf, London, 1989. Sketch of stage III landscaping for Richard Rogers Partnership.

House, London. Conservatory.

Far left:House, London, 1975-6. Covered walkway from street entrance through landscaped courtyard to house entrance.

Holland   Vera Yanovshtchinsky

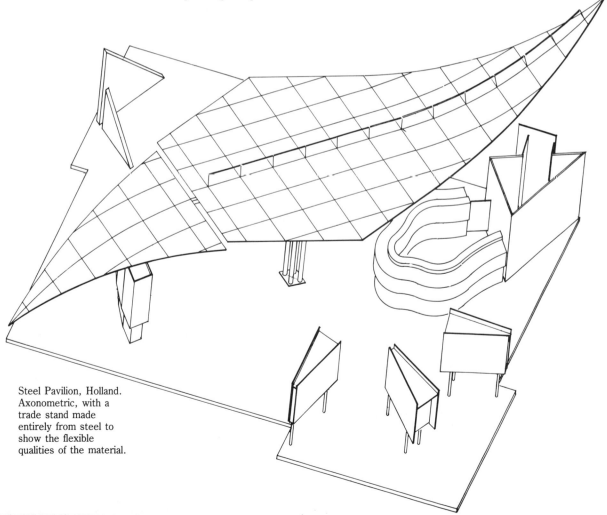

Vera Yanovshtchinsky

Biography
Born in Lvov, U.S.S.R. , in
1952, emigrated to Israel,
1960, came to Holland in
1975. Educated at the
Technicon, Department of
Architecture, Haifa, Israel,
1972-4 and at the Technical
University, Delft, 1975-83,
graduating with honours in
1983.
Vera Yanovshtchinsky has
been a partner of Homan,
Osorio Lobato,
Yanovshtchinsky,
Architeketn-Maatschap, in
the Hague, since 1988.
From 1986-8 she ran her
own office, and worked for
Jan Brouwer Associates and
Atelier Pro in the Hague,
and Lucas en Ellerman in
Voorburg. She is a
committee member of the
Berlage Stichting, the
Hague, 1986-, and a
member of the
Weltstandcommissie, 1987-,
which oversees the quality
of buildings and public
spaces in the Hague. She
teaches at the Royal
Academy of Fine Arts, the
Hague, 1988-.
Selected work:
Conversion of a seventeenth
century building into a
music auditorium,
Middleburg, Holland, 1986-
9. Restaurant,
Scheveningen, 1987.
Restaurant/pavilion, the
Hague, 1987. 74 dwellings at
s' Gravenzandelaan, the
Hague, 1988-90. Artist
supplies store, the Hague,
1989. 45 single family

'As an architect one is asked to create physical and functional conditions for particular needs,' reflects Vera Yanovshtchinsky. 'I have to see the task in a broader context, as a story. In addition to definition and description the ''Story'' must leave sufficient space for the unknown - for individual interpretation and expectation. The ''Story'' is inspired by tangible matters such as programme, the urban plan, location, technical feasibility and so on, and also by abstract parameters such as culture, history and vision of the future. Together they must be cohesive and show inner consistency.'

'I see my task as creating the architectural, environmental and functional setting within which the story can unfold. In doing so I have to keep certain aspects in mind, irrespective of the scale or significance of the project:
- to widen the functional concept by linking practical needs to spatial qualities.
- to weigh up the use of materials and construction techniques offered by modern technology.
- to relate architecture and urban planning components to each other so that they enrich one another.
- to include other disciplines, such as the visual arts, in a project.
I always hope that the result will show a synthesis of these points.'

'In practice I try to achieve this by combining my own design capabilities with those of others; architects, builders, designers, and visual artists.'

Vera Yanovshtchinsky worked with great pleasure in close co-operation with the artist Henia Eizenberg on her conversion of a seventeenth century listed building in Middleburg into a showcase for modern music, 1986-90.

Her pavilion for the Netherlands Steel Centre at the Utrecht building exhibition in 1987 shows her determination to exploit the characteristics of a material to the full. The pavilion's roof, which is made of perforated sheet steel, is balanced in equilibrium on steel columns and shows the flexibility, strength and freedom of form which the material offers.

Steel Pavilion, Holland.
Axonometric, with a
trade stand made
entirely from steel to
show the flexible
qualities of the material.

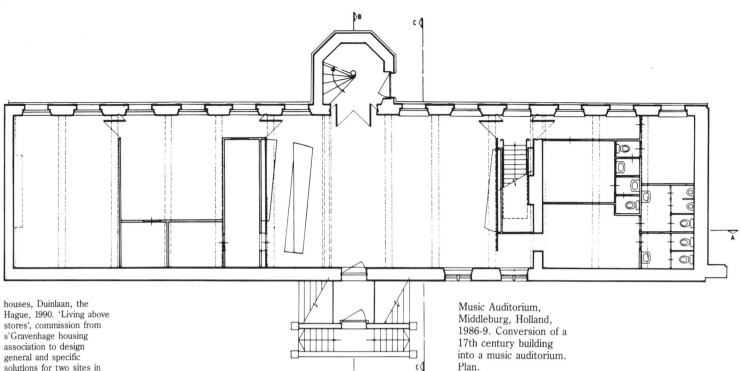

houses, Duinlaan, the Hague, 1990. 'Living above stores', commission from s'Gravenhage housing association to design general and specific solutions for two sites in the Hague, 1989-.

Awards:
First prize for the Middleburg music auditorium, 1986. Vera Yanovshtchinsky's work has been exhibited in Rotterdam, 1984, Florence, Italy, 1987, twice in the Hague, 1987, and also in 1989. Her work has been published in *de Architekt*, 1983, *Bouwen met Staal*, 1984, 1986, 1987, *Casabella*, 1987 and *Bouw*, 1988.

Music Auditorium, Middleburg, Holland, 1986-9. Conversion of a 17th century building into a music auditorium. Plan.

Music Auditorium. Interior door and window detail.

141

Reading list and references

The Grand Domestic Revolution, Dolores Hayden, MIT Press, 1982.

From Tipi to Skyscraper, Doris Cole, MIT Press, Cambridge, Mass, 1973.

Women in American History, edited by Susana Torre, Whitney Library of Design, New York, 1977.

AA Files No 18, A Picnic by the Roadside, or work in hand for the Future, Catherine Cooke on contemporary Soviet architects, Architectural Association, London, Autumn 1989.

AA Files No 15, Charlotte Perriand, Mary McLeod, 1988.

Blueprint, article on contemporary Australian architecture and interiors by Sudjic, Quarry and Jackson, London, September, 1988.

The Independent, leader on women's average earnings, London, 25 Jan 1989.

Architects' Journal, RIBA membership under 40 years old, London, 25 Jan 1989.

Intercity Magazine, report of male/female roles at work and home, 1989.

Women and the land – a suitable profession, Catherine Brown and others, Landscape Architecture, vol 72, no 3, London, May 1982.

RIBA enquiry into the lack of Women in Architecture, Neal Morris, Building Design, no 640, London, May 1983.

Women in Architecture, Eva Rudberg, Arkitektur, vol 83, Stockholm, March 1983.

A Woman's place, Annette Garland, no 664, June 1983, and Co-operating for change, no 648, Building Design, London, July 1983.

Women Architects in Denmark, Gertrude Galster, Arkitekten, vol 85, no 16, Copenhagen, 1983.

Women Architects in Finland, Kate MacIntosh, RIBA Journal, vol 90, no 9, London, 1983.

Do women design differently?, Jennifer Nicholls, Architect, vol 7, no 2, Melbourne, 1983.

Getting an even deal for Women, Annette Garland, Building Design, vol 675, London, February 1984.

The New Ladies of Building, Francis Rambert, Architectes, no 142, Paris, November 1983.

Celebrating Women, exhibition of Women's architecture at the RIBA reported in Architects' Journal, vol 179, no 10, London, 1984.

Architecture – work by women, Nancy Patterson in Fifth Column, Toronto, Summer 1983.

Girls get rights to jobs for the boys, report on US Supreme Court Judgement on sex discrimination in partnership appointments, Building Design, no 685, London, June 1984.

Lux Guyer, first Swiss woman architect, Rita Schiess, Aktuelles Bauen, November 1983.

A Woman's Place, Grace Pieniazek, Building, London, September 1984.

Women Architects in the UK, Monica Pidgeon, Progressive Architecture, vol 65, no 10, 1984.

Chicago Women in Architecture, 1974 – 84, Sabra Clark and others, Inland Architect, USA, November 1984.

Working Relationships, report on male/female partnerships, Bauwelt, March 1985.

Equal career opportunities?, Naomi Rosh White, Architecture Australia, March 1985.

Gender, culture and architectural values, Suzanne Estler and others, Crit, no 13, Autumn 1983.

Austrian Women Architects, U.I.F.A. presentation in Paris 1983 and Berlin 1984, Sundt and Filas, Aufbau, vol 40, no 2, 1985.

Itsuko Hasegawa, Suzuki and others, Space Design, no 247, Japan, 1985.

Tindale bows out, Alan Thompson, Building Design, no 778, London, 1986.

Industry role for women, Karen Brown, report on the Women in Professions, conference at the RIBA, Building, no 7483, London, 1987.

Women architect wins compensation in equality action, John Wood, Building Design, no 839, London, 1987.

Der Bauch der Architektin, Marina Duttman and others, Bauwelt, West Germany, October 1987.

Built by Women, guide to architecture by women in the New York area, 1981.

That Exceptional One, exhibition of work by women architects from 1888 – 1988, touring in the USA, 1988 – 90.

Ladies First, exhibition of the work of 40 Swiss women architects, Zurich 1987. Reviewed in the Zurich Tagblatt des Radt, February 1987.

Progressive Architecture, reader poll on women in architecture, October 1989.

Women in Design, Design, no 485, London, 1989.

The Future is Female, American Express Expression magazine, September 1989.

Mother's Work, review by Nan Stone in the Harvard Business Review, Sept/Oct 1989, of The Second Shift by Arlie Hochschild, Viking, 1989, and Women's Quest for Economic Equality by Victor Fuchs, Harvard University Press, 1988.

1988 Survey of R.A.I.A. members.

Women in the Architectural Profession report by the R.A.I.A. to the Human Rights Commission, 1986.

Statistics on Women members, A.I.A. Archive of Women in Architecture.

Board of Architects of New South Wales, statistics on membership, 1922 – 88.

Architects Board of Western Australia, statistics on membership, 1922 – 89.

R.I.B.A. Marketing Department, membership statistics, 1911 – 89.

40 under 40, R.I.B.A. exhibition catalogue, 1988.

Associations started by, and for, Women Architects.
International:
Union Internationale des Femmes d'Architecture. (U.I.F.A.)
Sweden:
Athena, started in 1986, 300 members, based in Stockholm.
Women's Building Forum.
Finland:
Arkitekta, started circa 1950 in Helsinki.
Australia:
Constructive Women, an association for women architects, town
planners and landscape architects, started in Sydney in 1982.
Britain:
R.I.B.A. Women Architects Group.
Holland:
Stichtung Vrouwen Bouwen en Wonen, Rotterdam.
West Germany:
Frauen Organization fur Plannerinnen und Architektinnen, West
Berlin.
Switzerland:
Ladies Forever, based in Zurich.

Statistics

It is a commonly held view that as the number of women entering the architectural profession grew enormously in the 1970s and 1980s no difficulties face - or will face - those young women who choose to become architects.

The underlying argument is that in those professions where there has traditionally been low representation of one gender or the other, improvements in the workplace are inevitable if the under-represented sex increases in numbers.

I wished to test whether there has indeed been an explosion of women architects, and to chart their rise, by looking at the numbers registered as female members of the profession. I soon found this was easier said than done.

Most countries, when asked for figures about the number of women in the architectural profession during the last forty years were unable to respond due to inadequate record keeping on the part of national registration councils or architectural bodies. There was however a response from the countries listed below, and although the figures are not directly comparable they are the best that are available.

AUSTRALIA
Architects are registered in each of the 8 states or territories. The Royal Australian Institute of Architects cannot sort members historically by gender.
Board of Architects of New South Wales

	women members	total members	% women members
1923-59	76	no figure	no figure
1923-89	326	3 191	10.2

Architects Board of Western Australia

1922-59	10	331	3.0
1965	12	465	2.6
1975	18	746	2.4
1985	28	1,022	2.7
1922-89	39	1,226	3.2

BRITAIN
The Architects' Registration Council of Great Britain cannot sort members by gender, however the Registrar thought that the following applied as a rough guide:

1989	3,000	30,000	10.0

Royal Institute of British Architects

1922-59	453	8,437	5.4
1955	369	6,314	5.8
1965	549	11,687	4.7
1975	857	19,014	4.5
1985	1,395	26,315	5.3
1922-89	1,768	29,148	6.1

In contrast, the industrial design profession in Britain boasted 2% women members in 1988 (20% in Japan), while in graphic design 42% (in Britain) were women.

HOLLAND
Bond van Nederlandse Architekten, Amsterdam. Government Architect's Registration Bureau, The Hague. No access to data.

Records of state registered architects started in 1988 upon computerization.

NORWAY
Norske Arkitekters Landsforbund, Oslo. Approximately 80% of registered architects are members of the N.A.L.

1955	88	902	9.6
1965	118	1,249	9.4
1975	189	1,697	11.1
1985	380	2,609	14.6
data from another source:			
1989	no figure given	2,820	19.0

SPAIN
No official figures from the Colegio Oficial de Arquitectos (State registration body), however the Hermandad Nacional de Arquitectos produced the following:

1955	no records	no records	no records
1965	12	2,254	0.5
1970	40	3,285	1.0
1975	144	5,784	2.5
1983	664	13,307	5.0

UNITED STATES
U.S. Census Bureau, which includes registered architects, planners, architectural and interior designers in a single category.

1975	3,010	70,000	4.3
1980	6,030	90,000	6.7
1984	11,556	107,000	10.8

American Institute of Architects

1955	123	10,634	1.2
1965	184	17,925	1.0
1975	240	24,144	1.0
1985	1,467	48,742	3.0
1989	2,369	53,142	4.5

INTERNATIONAL ACADEMY OF ARCHITECTURE

1988	0	40	0

ENTRY TO ARCHITECTURAL SCHOOLS.
In a number of countries a positive discrimination policy operates to increase opportunites for female students to enter architectural schools.

AUSTRALIA. No nationally agreed affirmative action. Royal Australian Institute of Architects Education Division.

	women students	total students	% women students
1974	no figure	no figure	9.3
1984	"	"	18.3
1987	"	"	27.5

BRITAIN. No nationally agreed affirmative action.
Royal Institute of British Architects.

1985	"	"	24.1
1986	"	"	25.2
1987	"	"	28.8

At the Architectural Association School of Architecture the following figures applied to first year entry students:

	women students	total students	& women students
1966	10	75	13.3
1976	8	57	14.0
1986	18	58	31.0
1987	22	45	48.9

(Teaching staff, part and full time, at the A.A. school were as follows:

	women staff	total staff	% women staff
1988	18	107	16.8

None of the full time staff were women.)

NORWAY. Affirmative action at Oslo and Trondheim schools, none at Bergen. At Bergen the intake of students was as follows:

	women students	total students	% women students
1988	18	28	64.3

The 3 schools combined produced the following:

1988	no figure	no figure	55.0

UNITED STATES
Affirmative action policies at most schools. No official figures, but the percentage of women entering the first year at several well known schools was thought to be around 40% in 1989.